£8-45

MANAGING PRIMARY SCHOOLS
A Professional Development Approach

MANAGING PRIMARY SCHOOLS
A Professional Development Approach

Christopher Day
David Johnston
Patrick Whitaker

Harper & Row, Publishers
London

Cambridge
Philadelphia
New York
San Francisco

Mexico City
São Paulo
Singapore
Sydney

Copyright © Christopher Day, David Johnston and Patrick Whitaker
All rights reserved
First published 1985

Harper and Row Ltd
28 Tavistock Street
London WC2E 7PN

130929

British Library Cataloguing in Publication Data

Day, Christopher
    Managing primary schools: a professional
    development approach.
    1. Elementary schools—Great Britain—
    Administration
    I. Title   II. Johnston, David   III. Whitaker,
    Patrick
    372.12'00941   LB2822.5
    ISBN 0–06–318306–4

370.7942
DAY

0028361

Typeset by Inforum Ltd, Portsmouth
Printed and bound by Butler & Tanner Ltd, Frome and London

CONTENTS

INTRODUCTION

The primary stage of British education has never been short on imagination. Even its most severe critics would have to acknowledge that there has hardly been a time, since the 1870s, when the 'leitmotif' of zest and creativity has not been detectable in some part of the country. Cynics might attribute such imagination simply as being a by-product of working with the more easily stimulated, adult-oriented, pre-pubertal child. Organization theorists might see it as in part resulting from ease of intimacy and communication in a system of predominantly small schools (average staff in 1986 is 7+). The reality is much more complex, a subtle mixture of the two elements mentioned combined with a history of determined (and at times dogged) commitment from staff, inspectorate and teacher-trainers to what Blyth once called a 'primary', rather than an 'elementary', perspective, which he and others later expanded in terms of the 'enabling curriculum' (Blyth 1984).

In the 1980s, throughout western education, the cult of utility is paramount. At its worst this becomes translated into the view that, 'That which cannot be quantified, or seen as capable of yielding a profit, is not real.' Words like creativity, happiness and interest no longer command respect in the courts of the administrators. Education must be seen to get you somewhere, preferably to get the country as a whole into an era of prosperity. Yet, despite this, the primary schools of the western world do not knock up against the dole queue, against commerce, against industry, in quite the brutal and contingent way in which secondary schools do in times of economic recession. In short, whilst knowledge, skills and values must be provided, *childhood* and its essential qualities of curiosity and excitement mercifully intervene. These qualities are still the catalysts to meaningful learning, and still so often the reasons why teachers accept erosion of status and salary, for they offer much that is humanizing and real, much that is lastingly rewarding, remaining in the mind long after the pronouncements of politicians and pundits have passed.

What, the reader may ask, has all this to do with the subject of this book? Everything, is the reply; for here is a book written by lovers of primary education, by practitioners mindful of the need to manage primary schools as professional, accountable, and yet essentially *educational* institutions. This is an account and a compendium blending theory with practice, research with prescription. It recognizes that school teaching is one of the 'caring professions' and seeks to examine how a school may best be run and evaluated. At the same time it is concerned to show that a good primary school is a humanizing, warm and supportive place where the quality of relationships between children, parents and teachers is of vital importance.

The other side of the picture perhaps needs emphasis too. Warmth is not enough; and haphazard learning is not likely to encourage systematic understanding or the growth of persistence and self-responsibility. Schools have a dual role, to serve society and to serve the individual. Each role must be sustained, examined, developed and assigned equal value. When the rhetoric of accountability and utility dies down, the balance of this dual role is still the collective responsibility of the Department of Education and Science, the local education authorities, the headteachers and individual class teachers. To this end, the enhancement of the teaching profession lies not only in its collective levels of control, supply and qualification, but in the serious study of the mechanisms of institutionalized education with a view to making these amenable to identification, understanding and possible agreement. In this way intuition and ideology are replaced by a proper combination of theory and practice. Whilst primary education may never have been short of imagination, it has never been short of ideology either; and frequently the latter has been confused with theory.

It is particularly important that small institutions dealing with the difficult-to-quantify 'production' of enlightened, considerate, reflective human beings should not be confused with large commercial establishments. It is seductive to attempt to translate 'line-management', 'productive work-force' and similar concepts straight into Merryfields Primary School! In the past the collective wisdom concerning management of secondary schools (with their staffs of ten times the size of that of the average primary school) has too often been added to commercial experience and then offered as a curious admixture to primary heads. In more recent years, experienced practitioners have began to rectify the glib translations and omissions of such packages. They have recognized the uniqueness of the British primary school, its smallness, its polymathic concerns, its less rigid classification and framing, its majority female staff. They have been at pains to emphasize that, whilst there are identifiable skills necessary in staff selection, there are also anxious parents leaving their four-year-olds for the first time – and known ways of alleviating that anxiety.

Leadership is a recurrent theme throughout this book; a leadership which recognizes the unique and independent traditions inherent in teaching; leadership which stresses that there is a delicate balance between maximizing institutional health and preserving that of the individual teacher. Changes in the patterns of recruitment, and relative stasis in career opportunities, combine with other wider social and political forces to make the role of leader somewhat more difficult than that implied in the old notices of legendary fame: 'Headteacher – do not disturb', 'Parents not allowed into the school without prior permission', and so on. To run a school is not quite as simple as some industrial barons would have us believe. Schools are not there merely to mould, certificate and grade; they are concerned with human development, with the welfare of a nation. Moreover, schooling occurs in a very public arena. Everyone is an expert; we have all been to school. There is no shortage of advice offered. The delicate balance between individual and societal needs is paralleled in that balance inherent in a curriculum which must provide for an unknown future and the dynamics of change as well as for a firm basis of cultural 'roots' and past experience. Thus the headteacher has many balancing acts to perform. He or she has to articulate and clarify ambiguities of social expectation to both parent and LEA. He or she must consult, modify and (perhaps) inspire those to whom 'the daily round, the common task' can at times seem pointless and undramatic.

Overall, I remain convinced that we in this country are extremely lucky to have such an expert, such a caring, such a democratic and such a hard-working teaching profession. Teachers deserve wholehearted support and interest. We should remember that they are frequently neglected, derided and (seemingly) deliberately misunderstood. Only when the leader has experience of the routines of such institutions of their peer-pressures, happiness, insolence, surprise, resentment, noise and anxiety; only when that leader manages from a certain sure basis of empathy and expertise, can the professionalism emerge which takes a school forward into the future.

What follows here is offered as part of that process of extended professionalism. It is based on reflection and research tempered by observation and experience. In all this we should remember that there are few absolutes. Schools, as units of analysis, are rather like people – infinitely different. Like people they can grow or decay. This book is an attempt to establish a sound basis for continued school and hence professional growth.

Philip Gammage, 1985
University of Nottingham

Blyth, W.A.L. (1984) *Development, Experience and Curriculum in Primary Education*, London, Croom Helm.

CHAPTER 1

LEADERSHIP AND CONSULTANCY: AN ACTION-CENTRED PERSPECTIVE

This chapter considers the headteacher first and foremost as a leader of adults, with responsibility for ensuring opportunities for staff learning which are related both to individual and school needs. These will be of different kinds at different times, since staff, like children, will be at different stages of development. The complexity of leadership and consultancy roles is recognized and the chapter offers practical assistance in planning and reflecting on the task of leadership in which the head acknowledges that staff have an active part to play in their own learning and thus the management of the school.

In the ever increasing number of texts concerned with management, the most neglected area is often the process of management itself. There seems to be an assumption that once aims, objectives and means of assessment have been clarified all that has to be done is to follow a series of prescribed steps, or to complete a checklist; or at another extreme that leaders (or managers) must already possess the necessary qualities and skills or they would not be leaders! Those who have experienced leadership roles will know that prescribed checklists for action are fallible and that opportunities for teachers to develop management skills are even now few and far between.

Before proceeding, it is necessary to define the notion of leadership which underpins this chapter and which is implicit in the book as a whole. Leadership here is defined as 'consultancy'. This enables us to think in terms of roles rather than 'positions'; and this in turn has the immediate effect of focusing on people and purposes. The objective of this chapter, therefore, is to explore how all those (including headteachers) who wish to influence others might do so most effectively. Emphasis will be laid on particular processes of consultancy by leaders, rather than on the particular strict occupational role which different leaders might hold. In this way both the needs of leaders in 'managing' and the needs of staff who are being 'managed' will be considered.

> By the consulting process, I mean any form of providing help on the content, process, or structure of a task or series of tasks, where the consultant is not actually responsible for doing the task itself[1] but is helping those who are. The two critical aspects are that help is being given, and that the helper is not directly responsible within the system (a group, organization or family) for what is being produced. Using this definition, consulting is a function, not an occupational role per se.
> (Steele 1975)

[1] Anything a person, group or organization is trying to do.

The consultant, be he or she head, deputy, scale-post holder, or LEA Adviser/Inspector, can only be *indirectly* responsible for the teaching in the classroom, for he or she is dealing with adults with their own perceptions of their responsibilities. Adults, like children, cannot be developed; they can only be given opportunities to develop. This is a crucial principle, for it points the way to the consultant's role in the process of curriculum and staff development. In essence, he or she cannot enforce change, only promote it.

It must be stated at the outset that the leader's job is first and foremost to influence others in order to ensure maximum efficiency and effectiveness of the teaching – learning process. In the case of primary-school headteachers, the people they must influence are the staff, the children, the parents, the school managers and the LEA. Although each of these groups will influence the headteacher, only he or she is in a position to have an overview which takes into account each of the needs expressed, but which is more than their sum. This is expected of a leader and is variously called a policy, an ideal, a set of aspirations or a vision for the school which the head holds and is expected to communicate to all the interest groups which make up a school community. Figure 1.1 is a simple representation of the head in the centre of a very complex communications network.

The network is complex because between groups and within each group there will be expectations, demands and abilities which may conflict. The head will need to identify and balance these interests before decisions are made, wherever possible taking into account the different influences at work and the consequences of accepting one at the expense of another.

How effectively and efficiently this network operates, depends on the

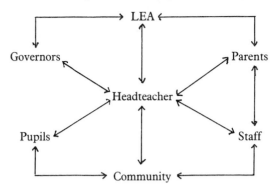

Figure 1.1   The head at the centre of the communications network

head's ability to receive and interpret signals accurately, to ensure communication within and between groups and to influence one or more of the groups. The head is regarded by all groups as the focal point of school life – with the possible exception of the pupils, who may regard their class teacher in this way. Indeed, a useful analogy may be drawn here, for, like the class teacher, the head has to ensure that his or her 'audience' feels secure (through good organization and an environment conducive to learning), feels able to contribute (to their own learning, and, hence, feeling of self-worth), feels able to communicate (through the building of satisfactory working/professional relationships), and feels a sense of continuity and progression (through the head's ability to monitor and assess progress). So it is the way in which the head intervenes in the lives of these groups which is crucial to his or her success in influencing them.

Action-centred leadership

Anyone who has been involved in leadership will know that there can be enormous discrepancies between what has been called the logic of planning and the logic of action (Stake 1967). In the action of managing even the best-laid plans may go astray.

Below is a fine example, from an industrial context, of the logic of rational planning for action-centred leadership. It is suggested that there are interrelated purposes for the action-centred leader – developing individuals, achieving the task and building the team; and it is implied that there are 'action points' for putting these purposes into practice.

1. Set the task of the team; put it across with enthusiasm and remind

people of it often.

2. Make leaders accountable for 4-15 people; instruct them in leadership actions.
3. Plan the work, check its progress, design jobs and arrange work to encourage the commitment of individuals and the team.
4. Set individual targets after consulting; discuss progress with each person regularly, but at least once a year.
5. Delegate decisions to individuals. If not, consult those affected before you decide.
6. Communicate the importance of everyone's job; explain decisions to help people apply them; brief the team together monthly on progress, policy, people and points of action.
7. Train and develop people, especially the young; gain support for rules and procedures, set an example and 'have a go' at those who break them.
8. Where unions are recognized, encourage joining, attendance at meetings, standing for office and speaking up for what each person believes is in the interest of the organization and all who work in it.
9. Serve people in the team and care for their wellbeing; improve working conditions and safety; work alongside people; deal with grievances promptly and attend social functions.
10. Monitor action; learn from success and mistakes; regularly walk round each person's place of work, observe, listen and praise.

(The Industrial Society 1983)

These stages of action are clearly relevant to leaders in primary schools in their planning, but in considering their actions it is necessary to uncover the value system and attitudes upon which this planning and action is based.

McGregor (1960) proposed two perspectives on management. He devised a 'Theory X' and 'Theory Y' view of human enterprise. Theory X:

McGregor postulates that workers become passive as a result of Theory X

> . . . is a conventional management perspective, which views people as needing to be directed, controlled and motivated, with their behaviour moulded to fit the needs of the organization. It reflects paternalistic and mechanistic approaches to management, which emphasize man's need for external pressures to 'keep him in shape' and combat his natural laziness and irresponsibility. Like a donkey, man works best with a conditioning mixture of the carrot (bribes) and the stick (threats). In practice, Theory X is exemplified in individual incentive schemes, clocking on, emphasis on discipline, and promotion based on length of service.

management. Theory Y, on the other hand, conceives of man as active by nature. Everyone has the potential for development, the capacity for responsibility and the readiness to direct their behaviour towards the goals of the organization. This is the participative approach in which work is seen as potentially satisfying in itself, because it is as natural an activity as playing. People only become passive and uncooperative because of their experiences, and it is a manager's job to remove obstacles and release potential. In practice, Theory Y is exemplified by agreeing targets, good delegation and job enrichment.

This book, whilst recognizing that there are occasions for adopting a Theory X approach, asserts that more effective leadership will occur through the use of a Theory Y view of management. We argue, for example, that in the case of the checklists and prescribed steps associated with Theory X, no account is taken of the attitudes to development held by the people with whom you have to work; nor their expectations, abilities, feelings, different processes of working. These will tend to get in the way of the appreciation of the 'grand plan' devised in the tranquillity of home or office. Theory X also implies that leaders or managers have acquired the necessary expertise to 'manage' adults. This is by no means necessarily so, since almost all headteachers and deputies will have spent most of their professional lives working with children, and not with the adults who now claim the major part of their time and attention.

Leadership or consultancy

Many people have attempted to classify leadership styles and to suggest which are the most effective. The best-known styles have been dubbed 'authoritarian', 'democratic' and 'laissez-faire' (Lippitt and White 1958), and while it is generally accepted that the last is the least effective there has always been disagreement about which of the other two is the more effective. The argument is often shelved by putting the difference down to the personality of the individual! Meighan (1981) identified styles of leadership by the class teacher which may usefully be applied to leadership of staff. He described two broad categories: authoritarian, where the pupils remain dependent on the teacher; and democratic, where pupils are interdependent with the teacher. Within each of these categories there were a number of orientations.

In figures 1.2 and 1.3, we have substituted 'teacher' for the original 'pupil' and 'leader' for 'teacher'. Each of the 'authoritarian' styles (Figure

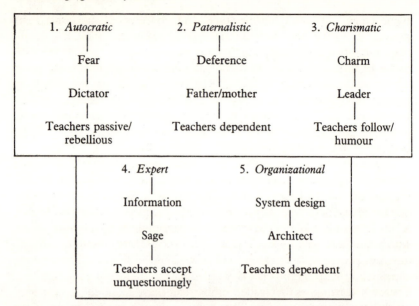

Figure 1.2   Authoritarian styles – teachers remain dependent on leader. *Source*: adapted from Meighan (1981) *A Sociology of Educating*, Holt Rinehart and Winston

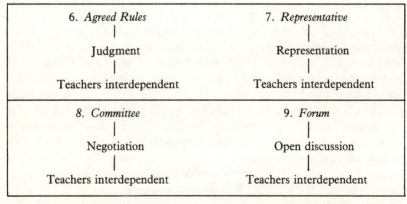

Figure 1.3   Democratic styles – teachers are interdependent with leader. *Source*: adapted from Meighan (1981) *A Sociology of Educating*, Holt Rinehart and Winston

1.2) is distinct, and each (with the exception of style 1) holds possibilities for movement towards the 'democratic' styles (Figure 1.3).

We are not seeking to make judgments on leadership effectiveness at this point. However, it is interesting to speculate on the possible cause-and-effect link between the authoritarian style of leadership and low self-expectations of teachers, who are rarely, if ever, called upon to participate in staff discussions on the shape of the curriculum or home-school policy, and who are not consulted about significant developments of any kind. Teachers in this position are unlikely to show initiative or feel confident in their own ability to engage in, for example, decision-making activities outside their own classrooms. In the first place they have had no practice, and secondly they may feel that it is not their responsibility. So it may be that the leader who consistently avoids involving others in planning and decision-making is actively teaching his or her staff to feel incompetent in these processes. Though working in a different context, Seligman (1975) identified this as 'learned helplessness'.

Professional relationships and motivation

What most influences teachers in schools? Below are a number of vignettes provided by headteachers in answer to this question. Each has been selected because it provides an example of a different quality of leadership in action, and of how teachers were motivated by processes of social influence. In particular, each teacher was helped by the head in processes of internalization, rather than in compliance or identification with authority or charisma. Change based on such compliance or identification is less likely to be long-term than change which accords with or may be adapted to the person's own value system (Kelman 1961).

Example 1: Timing (knowing when to help and when to let staff get on)

In my first year of teaching I had a problem with teaching mathematics. I knew what I wanted to teach but my organization was letting me down and producing a negative effect with my class. My headteacher noticed this without me having to go to him, showing an awareness of things going on in school and an awareness of the problems confronting new teachers. He suggested that he took my class for mathematics for a period of three weeks while I stayed in the classroom and watched.

From this I gained a good deal of knowledge about organization not only of mathematics but also of other subjects. His was a practical help which the situation needed initially and from then on gave advice when asked for or when he felt it necessary.

Example 2: Clear communication

The head in question was an excellent organizer. She knew what she wanted within the school and she made sure all the staff knew what was happening down to the last detail. This covered all aspects of school life, from organization of the curriculum to ordinary everyday events and the social life of the school. No member of staff likes to know they are being left in the dark; if they know what to expect they will respond positively.

Example 3: Practical empathy

A few years ago I was teaching in a large primary school where three teachers were serving a probationary year. These were young female teachers, all with quiet personalities. On the staff at the time were some rather forceful characters. The three young teachers were afraid to enter the staffroom at playtime (and admitted this). The headteacher concerned dealt with this by having small weekly meetings with them to discuss their problems, and the progress they were making. (As deputy head I was also involved.) This was in addition to helping them individually in classrooms, or with lesson plans and evaluation.

By being together, they felt more confident expressing opinions about their work. The sympathy shown by the head, by placing himself in their position, encouraged them to contribute in full staff meetings.

Example 4: Leading by example

The headteacher was very enthusiastic about the countryside and 'environmental studies'. He inspired others. A Bird and Tree Festival was held annually at which an invited speaker talked to the children. A tree or shrub was planted in the school grounds. All the classes prepared for the day by studying some aspect of the environment and a prize was awarded for the best class project. There was music, dance, verse, writing and creative activities. The headteacher worked hard to build up to the day and he, throughout the year, kept the school garden attractive and productive of fruits, vegetables and flowers. The school benefited tremendously from the interest radiated by the headteacher without whom none of this would have taken place.

Example 5: Supporting staff against external pressures

Several years ago, the school where I worked as scale 3 language consultant had a particularly obnoxious chairman of governors who thought a great deal of himself and very little of teachers. His manner towards teachers was hectoring and loud and he and I fell foul of each other during a course I was running in my own time. He made loud comments and suggestions and his presence and attitude were undermining my work.

The head arrived on the scene and summed it up. His choices were to support me and incur the displeasure and its consequences of the chairman, or to laugh it off and let me down.

He spoke very coldly to the man, saying, 'If you feel you can do this better, then please go ahead. That will give Mrs X the chance to go home and rest; she's done a full day's work already. Otherwise I'd suggest you leave the premises.'

He left, clearly furious. At the next governors' meeting the head tackled the man and gained the support of the other governors. A resolution was passed that *any* governor would only come to school after telephoning or by invitation and would never interfere with the work of the school.

The head had showed his integrity by supporting me, who would make little trouble for him, at the risk of offending someone who was likely to make a lot – and subsequently tried to.

Example 6: Caring about personal and professional needs

The head for whom I worked the longest was a fatherly, old-fashioned gentlemanly style of headteacher. I willingly served on his staff and loyally supported almost everything he did. In analysing why this was so, I've decided that it was because he genuinely cared about me as a person. He expressed interest, not only in my professional work, but also in the members of my family and in all my out-of-school activities. He always had time to listen. This concern, which applied equally to all members of staff, caused me to feel valued, and I gave my very best in response.

If effective leadership means the ability to achieve such a response from members of staff, that was an instance of it. Not perhaps a very dramatic situation but an 'effective' one.

Example 7: Setting standards

As a newly qualified teacher my head was seldom too busy to talk to me and would continue to discuss the matter in hand even when I was on playground duty, by doing the duty with me. He always displayed a sympathetic approach and was ready with encouragement and praise when he visited the classroom. If he thought I was doing something which didn't quite measure up to his requirements or standards, he would say so – but always in a friendly fashion. I never felt that I was being put down and I respected that. He wouldn't suffer fools gladly, but he did it in a pleasant fashion. He was rather of the 'old school' and valued scholarship and 'standards'. He urged me to continue my own education, night-school courses etc, in order to become better qualified. Although formal himself he accepted that teachers would try new ideas and methods, which he tolerated rather than really enthused over. This head was respected in the community and was liked by parents, children and staff.

As a new teacher I appreciated his listening ear and his readiness to devote time to me. I respected his judgments and I found his advice to be wise and practical. I valued him greatly as a colleague and later, as a friend.

Example 8: Supporting change

When first appointed as a deputy head I wanted to introduce a new maths scheme throughout the school as one did not exist at that time. I was given the opportunity by the headteacher of first of all going round other classes to see what they were doing currently in maths (he took my class during these times). Next, staff meetings were arranged where I could talk about the new maths scheme to the head and the staff.

Once general approval had been gained and costings carried out, the head agreed that the scheme should be introduced. The head had encouraged me in this venture throughout by enabling me to see what was needed and by backing the need for change (and taking the final decision to introduce the new scheme).

These examples show how teachers were *motivated* by various leadership styles and strategies. The main purpose of intervention by the leader is motivation. The heads of the schools concerned intervened in various ways in the teacher's professional development, and this motivated them. In work which is concerned with questioning the teacher's self-image, the nature of professional relationships is of prime importance. For example, changing one's teaching style may involve a temporary 'burden of incompetence' (Macdonald 1973), so that there will be a considerable need for psychological and moral support. Change must take into account matters such as anxiety, status and identity (Day 1981). Successful development requires more than rational planning and action. It requires a knowledge of, and allowance for, the way people feel. This 'affective' area is rarely made explicit in preparation for developmental work, yet the attitudes of teachers to the head or other consultant who intervenes in their professional lives are clearly vital to the success of the intervention.

How is the leader who intervenes perceived? Is he or she an authority or a threat? A 'process helper' or a judge with alien values? The answers to these questions will depend largely on the interpersonal relationships which are formed with colleagues, and these will in turn be determined by how much the leader is seen to take into account personal individual factors in his or her management of people.

In a survey conducted with sixty headteachers, the most commonly cited qualities of a good head were in the 'affective' area of the work, viz:

1. Sympathy towards the ideas of others.
2. Appreciation of others' points of view.
3. Understanding of and concern for others.
4. Compassion.
5. Approachability by staff, parents and children.
6. The ability to deal with problems as they arise and 'still have a smile'.

7. The ability to inspire trust and confidence.
8. Tolerance, especially of opposing ideas.
9. Tact.
10. Willingness to praise, and be seen to praise.
11. Humour.
12. The quality of being a good listener.
13. The ability to cope with opposition and unpopularity, as well as with support and encouragement.
14. The ability to know when to pressurize and when to stand off.
15. The capacity to be fair and just, and to be seen to be fair and just.
16. The ability to lead, to guide, to cajole when necessary, to be loyal and supportive of the staff, and to maintain enthusiasm despite any problems.

Few who read this list will be surprised, yet we must ask, how do heads gain and refine these qualities? There are still relatively few training opportunities in the field of interpersonal skills and helping others to increase professional effectiveness.

Intervention: constraints, purposes and processes

Most of the time, in working with children, teachers are not able to spend much time reflecting on why they do what they do. The main reasons for this are the number of children involved, and the time and energy available. Classroom decisions have to be made, and problems resolved, relatively quickly. Because of the nature of their work, teachers become socialized into acting in this way, with the theory which underlies each action almost always at an implicit level. (This may be part of the reason for teachers' common mistrust of 'theory' as they understand it, i.e. not related to practice.) Given that this is so, it would not be surprising if leaders who are or have been part of this apparently 'theoryless' environment, in which decisions are taken on the spot and solutions quickly found to 'cope' with emerging problems, behaved in a similar way in their work with other teachers. After all, they have rarely received any in-service preparation for their new roles. And yet, because the head will be dealing with fewer 'clients', and because often decisions about development or change do not need to be taken on the spot, the leader has more opportunity to reflect, and evaluate.

Since much teaching behaviour is at an intuitive and implicit level (we all have a 'filter system' in order to cope with the masses of information with which we have to deal), from time to time teachers need the help of a colleague from outside in identifying both areas of strength and areas for improvement. Often the headteacher fulfils this role, by means of the following:

1. Taking an 'overview' of the needs of the school as a whole.
2. Observing and working alongside individual teachers.
3. Providing the means by which the practice of individuals and the school may be monitored and reviewed.
4. Ensuring commitment of staff through participation in decision-taking.

The headteacher who observes his or her teachers at work in their classrooms, who encourages them to discuss their work with each other and him or herself at regular meetings with groups and individuals, will soon get to know the various stages of professional development reached by each of the teachers. Thus, having established a context for the learning, the head will be in a position to plan for the most effective means of motivating through a series of purposeful intervention strategies – purposeful in the sense that his or her perceptions of institutional need, which may be in potential conflict with those of the staff, can be modified in the light of systematically collected evidence of perceived staff need. So desired results may be achieved by thinking of the intervention strategies not only in terms of the task, but also in terms of human motivation and learning factors. (A detailed discussion of these is contained in Chapter 4.) While these learning factors will be specific to the individual, there are general psychological needs which may be identified.

One way to help teachers is by identifying how and why they learn. It has been suggested that teachers are motivated to learn when they (rather than others) identify a need or problem. Havelock (1973) presented problem-solving as a rational process (Figure 1.4).

It is clear from the model in Figure 1.4 that identifying and solving problems is a complex business. For example, the initial disturbance may come from a self-generated or from an externally generated source (e.g. a new headteacher, a missive from the LEA, a visit by a colleague to the classroom, or simply a knowledge that all is not well). The feeling of need which arises may or may not be strong enough to warrant a decision to act. Indeed, the teacher may feel unable or unworthy to do something about the need, until and unless it is diagnosed as a problem. Even if the need is diagnosed as a problem, teachers may be inhibited in their search for

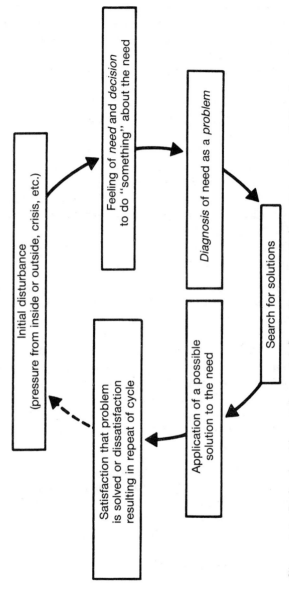

Figure 1.4 Rational problem solving model. *Source:* Havelock (1973) *The Change Agents Guide to Innovation*, Education Publications

solutions by lack of time, energy, ability, resources or skills. Clearly, the leader has a responsibility to ensure that teachers do have opportunities to reflect on their work, as well as to help them in identifying problems by providing alternative perspectives on their work. (For problems in introducing new ideas see Chapter 5.)

It should not be assumed, however, that *all* adults have a need to be self-directing at all times. Some teachers, like some children, may need to be 'told' things on occasion, or may expect that they should be told (a 'felt incompetence' formed by such factors as role, expectation, socialization or psychological needs – McGregor's 'Theory X'). Indeed, when teachers are participants in their own learning, problems may arise because their enquiry skills are either underdeveloped or undeveloped. The leader will need to take this into account. Among teachers, as among children, the need and ability to be self-directing will vary. 'Need', for example, depends upon factors such as cognitive and personality development, motivation, social development and role expectation.

The assumptions about professional learning and the nature of change which underpin the thinking expressed in this book are:

1. Professional development is not something that can be forced, because it is the teacher who develops (active), and not the teacher who is developed (passive) (Eraut 1977).
2. Change which is not internalized is likely to be distorted and temporary. Hence, power-coercive strategies or external initiatives which rely on authority rather than encourage development may seem to work, but usually result in 'token' changes at surface level only.
3. Change at deeper levels involves the modification of perceptions and attitudes, and this is unlikely to occur unless there is participation in the decision-making and planning of the in-service activity.
4. The leader's role is consultative and collaborative.

Many people have suggested that teachers in schools will work most happily and effectively in an environment to which they feel they belong (how many times do we hear the teacher talk of 'my class' and the head talk of 'my school'!), with which they can identify and in which they feel accepted and esteemed – not only by their pupils, but also by colleagues and their heads. Perhaps the prime task of the consultant/leader concerned with motivating staff is to provide the right conditions for motivation.

Leading the team

Like an individual, a team must be led in ways which take account of its stage of development as well as the purposes of the leader. The 'leader' needs to be able to:

1. Identify the team's stage of development.
2. Be aware of the range of approaches available to him or her.
3. Select the appropriate approach, according to the team's stage of development and the leader's purposes.
4. Possess and be able to use the ability to put this approach into practice.
5. Monitor the effectiveness of the approach, and modify where necessary.

In the ideal and most effective model of leadership the head's role is collaborative and he or she will operate according to principles of participation, negotiation, trust and responsibility. The more the head 'tells' (makes the decisions and announces them) or 'sells' (through persuasion) the more he or she will demonstrate his or her use of authority and the less will be the personal investment of colleagues in the enterprise. The more the head 'consults' (e.g. presents a problem, gets suggestions, makes decisions) or 'shares' (defines limits, asks group to make decisions), the greater will be the area of freedom felt by colleagues, and the stronger their investment. Whatever the question to be dealt with – whether it is to agree on a policy for staff development, or to review curriculum, or roles and responsibilities – it is crucial that the focus has been agreed through consultation so that all agree to commit themselves to the task in hand. The way in which this agreement occurs depends on the leadership roles adopted and the skills which can be applied.

In practice, the head who then operates any of the above models (with the possible exception of 'telling') will do so by means of talking, observing and listening. He or she will therefore need to possess and use a variety of skills necessary to the leading of effective discussion, and these will include:

1. Negotiating skills (contract-making).
2. Summarizing skills (to form links between different ideas, where appropriate).
3. Questioning skills (to open, rather than close discussions).
4. Selection skills (of key points in arguments).
5. Focusing skills (to concentrate and clarify discussion points).
6. Synthesizing and evaluation skills (to 'sharpen' issues).
7. Timing skills (to know when, and when not, to intervene in discussion).

8. Listening skills (to listen actively in order to respond to what is really being said – the hidden agenda).
9. Non-verbal skills (to identify people's attitudes and feelings, through observing posture, gesture, facial expression etc).

To summarize, in meeting with colleagues, either individually or collectively, the leader will need to demonstrate her ability to:

1. Negotiate sympathetically.
2. Listen (actively), note and act.
3. Account for individual needs.
4. Ensure continuity and support.
5. Send colleagues away with a sense of achievement.

Let us consider now four crucial factors in the process of management:

1. The needs of the individual and the needs of the institution

These may be different, and sometimes conflicting. Colleagues need to perceive the need for development (and thus change), and feel a responsibility for implementing and sharing in this. Individuals like to have responsibility and be trusted, but they also need to see benefits for themselves as well as for 'the school', for example. How may this be achieved? One way is by making social contracts with staff through negotiation. By these means, colleagues accept that they may at times, in the interests of others, contribute part of their autonomy. For example, the development of particular schemes of work may have to wait until there has been an appraisal of classroom teaching approaches. This 'contract-making' is often linked with the agreement to set different kinds of objectives according to agreed priorities. (See also Chapter 7).

2. Short/mid/long-term tasks

There may be some tasks better left until a later date because other tasks are more urgent, or because it is desirable for the staff to feel an immediate sense of achievement. So it is the head's responsibility to ensure that tasks are assigned different priorities. This is not to say that all three kinds of tasks are not being pursued at the same time, but simply that there is an agreement to place more emphasis at any given time on one rather than another.

3. Timing and containable time

Closely linked to these two factors is the concept of 'containable time'.

Changes must be manageable, and the time and energy which teachers have available to devote to change is limited. It is counterproductive to stretch people beyond their personal limits. Through initial contract-making, agreements can be reached concerning the amount of time to be spent on any given task or project. The knowledge that a meeting or other event will end at a given time will provide security for staff with other commitments.

A personal sense of timing is also important. Friday afternoon three or four weeks into term, or a wet and windy day which has unsettled the pupils in the school, may not be the best time to introduce a new idea!

4. Handling conflict

Inevitably conflict will occur from time to time, and the leader will be expected to handle it. There is no formula for success, but here are some notes drawn from the recent experiences of sixty deputy headteachers:

1. Provide support and guidance, i.e. identify the causes and try to eliminate or alleviate the problem through discussion/practical help and support.
2. Praise strengths and improvements.
3. Avoid open confrontation.
4. Offer positive 'professional' criticism.
5. Minimize feelings of being threatened.
6. Be prepared to accept modifications/compromise.
7. Avoid showing prejudice in open staff meetings if personal opinions are put forward.
8. Where you cannot handle conflict, be willing to use arbitration.

To these may be added a ninth:

9. Know which battles to fight, which to avoid, and which to lose!

Principles of consultancy-leadership

What qualities, then, do you need to possess in order to be an effective leader? First you have to recognize that you are involved in the management of human and physical resources. You have to help individuals to develop, while at the same time maintain the team. You must also ensure that the task, whatever it may be, is achieved. This will only happen if you can motivate and support others. *Management is getting things done with and by other people.* In order to do this well, you will need skills of planning and organization, in particular: identifying opportunities by being knowledgeable about the needs of staff and children, setting targets, the art of delegation and using your time to the best advantage; communication – formal and informal; assessment and evaluation – through monitoring, observing and synthesizing. Most important, then, are the skills of working with people. No amount of forward planning, careful budgeting or efficient administration can substitute for this.

One of the first principles-in-action for the consultant is participation by staff. This is based on the assumption that if people are involved in making the decisions that shape their activities, then they are likely to be more committed to their work. It is important to remember, though, that collectivity does not abolish the ultimate responsibility of the headteacher for the work of the school. The seven major areas of responsibility of the headteacher, each of which is dealt with in more detail in the other chapters in the book, are:

1. The school climate or ethos

It will be the head's policies regarding, for example, access to classrooms by parents, team teaching, a policy of professional development which is school-focused, the use of reward and punishment systems, the collegiality of school decision-making, which will determine whether the school is perceived as 'open' or 'closed' by staff and parents.

2. Organizational health — teaching and learning processes

What does the way in which school and classrooms are organized 'say' about the school? Is there a predominance of class teaching, individual work? Are the classroom doors usually open or closed?

3. The framework/expectations (standards of behaviour and achievement)

What are the standards of the school? Is there a high level of commitment by staff and children to providing a stimulating environment for learning? Is there an effective monitoring system for children's work? Is there a regular monitoring of staff's work? Are there regular head–staff, staff–staff, staff–parent, head–parent consultations?

4. Routines (morale)

Are there frameworks of routines for staff and children in school? Are there regular, organized staff seminars, appraisal interviews, meetings with parents, professional development opportunities?

5. Management of relationships

Leadership is a process, not a style. Constraints upon the processes are likely to be brought about by a number of factors. Some are outside the leader's control, i.e. national and local education policy. Some, however, are within the power of the head to influence:

Self   It is essential to have a strong professional philosophy. However, forceful expression of this may inhibit staff (who may not be so strong, clear-thinking or forthright), alienate staff, or inhibit the leader from acting in a collegial/democratic/consultative way with staff. Instead, the leader may resort to 'devious' manipulation which may in itself be counterproductive. Another problem for the leader is his or her isolation by status. It is difficult to share one's weaknesses, for example, with the person who is to write your reference!

Staff   It is unlikely that all the staff of a school will teach in the same way. Indeed it is questionable whether this should be so, except in the most general terms. However, it will be necessary to establish a unanimity of purpose for the school and to lead by example, avoiding the temptation to 'forcefeed'. The head should therefore:

(a) Create opportunities to develop unanimity from early success in an easy, non-controversial area, and limit change to single manageable areas but initiate changes fairly rapidly after initial assessment of needs.
(b) Establish consensus on problems – their recognition, analysis and resolution. Changes in management structure, for example, require a consensus of opinion in favour if they are to work.
(c) Give more thought to the operation to maximize contributions from all – this means plenty of preparation. Summarize discussion and record by written précis, ensuring continuous feedback to participants.
(d) Ensure acceptance by all team members that they may at times contribute best by surrendering part of their own autonomy, e.g. by accepting house rules in discussion and holding back criticism or interruption until the appropriate time.
(e) Identify motivation factors of each member of the team as individuals.

(f) Be aware of possible insecurities of staff (it is possible you may be carried away by your own enthusiasm).

(g) Ensure a commitment to the process rather than to the product of development.

(h) Establish a communication system which ensures truthful, honest and open assessment and evaluation.

6. *The curriculum*

The curriculum represents the knowledge that the school regards it as important that the students gain. In practice it is a mixture of tradition (the culture passed down by society), innovation (ideas developed by educationists) and basic skills development (numeracy and literacy). Increasingly curriculum is coming under public scrutiny and there are moves towards more public participation in its content. It is no longer enough to say that the head/leader must be aware of all major developments and ensure that the staff are aware of them. It is the effective management of the curriculum in relation to these developments which is vital, and this involves planning, monitoring and evaluating the content, the processes and the outcomes.

7. *Evaluation and assessment*

Whereas assessment of the pupils' work is an essential of every teacher's job evaluation of the work of individual teachers and the school as a whole is a prime responsibility of the headteacher. The purposes and practices of evaluation are considered in detail in Chapter 7, but run implicitly through all aspects of management practice. For example, evaluation will involve regular review of:

(a) Staff progress (see Chapters 3 and 4).

(b) The effectiveness of internal and external communications (see Chapters 5 and 8).

(c) The roles and responsibilities of staff (see Chapter 2).

(d) The curriculum (see Chapter 6).

How the head manages these evaluations determines his or her effectiveness.

Conclusion

This chapter has described a leader as one who provides environments which minimize constraints on learning, and where a variety of concrete experiences may be reflected upon, discussed, assimilated and accommodated; who involves others in identifying need, rather than identifying need for them; who matches, wherever possible, the perceived needs of the individual with the needs of the school as she perceives them. In working towards these ends, the leader will in effect be providing staff with access to and support from senior management; regular discussion with other professionals involved in education and other contexts; periods outside their classroom (and schools) to reflect upon practice; external professional knowledge and skills; and opportunities to establish and develop agreed and purposeful frameworks for their own roles.

References

Day, C.W. (1981) *Classroom-based In-Service Teacher Education: the Development and Evaluation of a Client-Centred Model*, University of Sussex Education Area, Occasional Paper no. 9.

Eraut, M.E. (1977) Strategies for Promoting Teacher Development, *British Journal of In-Service Education* vol. 4, nos. 1 and 2.

Havelock, R.G. (1973) *The Change Agent's Guide to Innovation*, Englewood Cliffs, New Jersey: Educational Technology Publications Inc.

Kelman, H. (1961) Three Processes of Social Influence, *Public Opinion Quarterly*, vol. 25, Princeton.

Lippitt, R. and White, R.K. (1958) An Experimental Study of Leadership and Group Life, *in* Maccoby et al. *Readings in Social Psychology*, Eastbourne: Holt, Rinehart and Winston.

Macdonald, B. (1973) Innovation and Competence, *in* Hamingson, D. (ed.) *Towards Judgement: The Publications of the Evaluation Unit of the Humanities Curriculum Project 1970-2*, Centre of Applied Research in Education, Occasional Publication no. 1, pp. 89-92.

Maslow, A.H. (1970 2nd ed.) *Motivation and Personality*, New York: Harper and Row.

McGregor, D. (1960) *The Human Side of Enterprise*, New York: McGraw-Hill.

Meighan, R. (1981) *A Sociology of Educating*, London: Holt, Rinehart and Winston.

Seligman, M.E.P. (1975) *Helplessness: on depression, development and death*, San Francisco: Freeman.

Stake, R.E. (1967) The Countenance of Educational Evaluation, *Teachers' College Record* vol. 68.

Steele, F. (1975) *Consulting for Organisational Change*, Amherst, Massachusetts: University of Massachusetts.

The Industrial Society (1983) *Action Centred Leadership*, London: Education for Industrial Society.

CHAPTER 2

ROLES AND RESPONSIBILITIES

Management in primary schools, as in most organizations, is about getting things done. Managers should be judged by the outcomes they facilitate rather than by the quality of their plans and policies. This chapter will explore some of the implications of this principle, suggesting that the present method of operating scale-post responsibilities in primary schools can inhibit effective management and stifle dynamic school development. The chapter builds on the assumption made in Chapter 1 that effective management is about teamwork and shared leadership, the working with and through all members of the staff group. As an alternative to the somewhat individualized approach to responsibility currently practised, two alternative models are offered, both of which provide the basis for a more cohesive team approach.

The present scalepost structure within primary schools has developed over the years by a process of accretion. Large schools have benefited most, with scale 3 posts available as well as scale 2. Small schools have been largely untouched by these developments although in recent years there have been attempts to provide some opportunity for heads in small schools to be relieved of some of their class responsibilities. In recent years, with declining pupil numbers, there has been a steady erosion of the scale-post structure as through succeeding triennial reviews schools have fallen into lower groupings, forfeiting scale points and posts.

This piecemeal growth and recent decline have meant that schools have used scale posts in a somewhat haphazard way. Although reporting committees like Bullock (DES 1975) and Cockcroft (DES 1982) have urged the designation of teachers as curriculum consultants in language and mathematics, there has been no concerted attempt to offer to schools an overall plan for scale-post allocation. Some schools have developed a structure of posts which is linked to a cohesive staff development programme, but generally speaking the pattern is inconsistent.

One of the factors that has contributed to this haphazard pattern is the assumption that once individual posts are designated they cannot be changed. It is true that teachers have protection from arbitrary changes to the terms and conditions of their contract, but there has never been a formal problem about change through mutual agreement. This tradition of immutability is now changing and many heads, working through participatory management, are involving teachers in the design of the post structure and in the redefining of roles and responsibilities.

Another factor, connected with the point made at the beginning of the chapter about managers being judged on performance, is that teachers themselves have tended to want to stay with those responsibilities with which they feel most safe – i.e. they see themselves as being judged on performance, and so are only happy with those responsibilities which they are confident of being able to fulfil. This has inhibited the creative use of scale posts to assist staff development. Posts have been associated with the idea of delivery rather than acquisition since teachers have been appointed for what they already are rather than for what they have the potential to become. Many curriculum-development projects and school innovation programmes might have been more successful if the scale posts relating to them had incorporated an element of staff development.

Staff mobility has also affected the issue. The tendency has been to replace like with like so that a scale-post-holder moving out of the school is replaced with another teacher who can carry the same or a very similar responsibility. The vacating of a post always creates an opportunity for reconsidering the structure and considering whether a programme of redefinition and reallocation can better help the staff as a team to respond to changing needs and circumstances.

One of the underlying beliefs that has helped to perpetuate the pattern of scale posts has been that of balance and coverage. Heads often talk about needing a teacher to 'cover' a particular curriculum area and of wanting to spread the curriculum between the number of scale posts available. It is also the case that deputies, and heads themselves, are often left out of such an allocation.

All these factors have contributed to a system that has failed to serve the best interests of schools and of the teachers who work in them. They have tended to create a dividing element rather than a unifying one. By separating out responsibilities we are forcing scale-post-holders to work for the realization of their own individual goals rather than those of the school as a whole. What happens in practice is that scale-post-holders have to try and influence each other, in order to further their individual aims. The existence of many individual plans and many separate programmes is both confusing and divisive.

An improved scale-post structure will be one which develops teamwork, facilitates group management and creates opportunities for leadership to emerge. It will also be one which utilizes and develops the personal and professional qualities of the staff. By linking the scale-post structure to a staff development policy it will be possible to facilitate professional development through some form of job rotation and team responsibility.

In addition to these factors it will also be necessary to develop a structure which has the flexibility to respond easily to new needs and changing circumstances. This suggests an underlying assumption that change in schools is a continuous process rather than a series of incidents or events. Regular curriculum and policy reviews will generate the awareness which will inform this process and provide the focus for teamwork and group management. The next part of this chapter examines the constraints which may prevent these conditions being achieved; and it looks at two models which attempt to overcome these and establish a truly collegial structure of roles and responsibilities.

Roles and responsibilities: constraints and possibilities

Our traditional pattern of roles and responsibilities in the primary school is locked within a system that regards a division of labour as essential. The head is seen as undertaking significantly different work from the class teacher, and between these two come a variety of roles, each with their different and distinct purposes. This pattern has been encouraged by the steady increase in the number of scale posts available in primary schools, and a belief that curriculum consultancy has the potential to improve the quality of learning inside classrooms. Recent proposals about a new structure for the teaching service revealed an acceptance that this pattern of curriculum specialization was not only against the best interests of primary teachers but that it was not achieving what had been hoped for it. Indeed the HMI survey of primary schools, published in 1978, observed:

> In a quarter of the schools in the survey teachers with positions of curricular

organizational responsibility were having a noticeable influence on the quality of the work in the school as a whole. In the remaining schools there was little evidence that the influence of teachers with curricular responsibilities spread beyond the work of their own classes.

Although this revelation shocked many at the time of its publication, 25 per cent of teachers exercising influence beyond their own classrooms is a remarkable achievement given the limited time and opportunity they have to undertake such work. Within the education service there has been a determination to try and improve the skills and abilities of scale-post-holders, mainly through in-service training. This is misguided. Carving up the curriculum into manageable chunks and distributing them to individual members of staff, asking them to go round influencing each other, is no recipe either for improving the quality of pupil learning or for achieving a more effective management structure.

The kind of management structure more likely to be successful in meeting the challenges of the future is one that makes optimum use of the human resources at its disposal. This will not only require the skilful combining of individual strengths and abilities but a capacity to build group and partnership skills within the working team. Staff development is often regarded as a process relating to the individual's particular professional needs. In the school of tomorrow it should also include a consideration of the needs of the staff as a whole. Leadership needs to be seen as a key function of the group and not only as the responsibility of a named individual. This need not diminish the role of the head. If anything it enhances it, creating new opportunities for working through and with a cohesive and committed team.

Such a structure is easier to conceive of than it is to achieve in practice, so it is important to be aware of the factors that currently work to inhibit the movement towards this more functional pattern. Foremost among these are the traditional assumptions affecting our work as teachers in an institutionalized education service.

Traditional assumptions

One of the reasons that teachers have found it so hard to respond to a more participatory style of school management is that such a model contradicts many of the established values of the schooling process. Teachers, like pupils, have been trained to follow and to occupy roles defined and structured for them by others. Within these prescribed roles of class teacher, deputy head or headteacher there is a tendency to be conditioned by the traditional orthodoxy displayed in the expectations that society has of its schools and its teachers. Many of the new generation of primary headteachers have gained their appointments because they have subscribed to an open and participatory managing style only to find that they are faced by a staff who have not. The problem often lies not with the headteachers but with the staffs they are appointed to lead, who have not had the same opportunities to develop an awareness of new possibilities. (See Chapter 5).

Education is plagued by mistake-avoidance. Pupils are trained to believe that not only must they get it right but that they must get it right first time. This ethic establishes itself early in the schooling process and becomes self-perpetuating. It has taken the computer to help us to realize that effective learning can be about getting it wrong first, and that the path to success need not be painful. The same ethic pervades the teaching profession, so that we have come to believe that there is one right way to do things and, rather than search for our own version of what that might be, we incline to the traditional, well-established and respected patterns where the possibility of censure and misfortune is at its least.

The last twenty or so years in education have witnessed a concern for curriculum development. This has emerged in the belief that if only we can get the design of what is taught in schools right most of the problems of education will be solved. This assumption has generated a view that the most desirable management activity in schools is changing things. Some heads seem to be preoccupied with the concept of the ultimate innovation. There is a belief that if change is approached systematically and painstakingly the school can be put on a sure footing that will support its activities for the foreseeable future. This is both to misunderstand the nature of change in schools and also to fail to appreciate that curriculum review can no longer be an occasional activity in schools but has to be a continual process. Instead of wanting our changes in school to be everlasting we need to see the challenge more as one of improving things for the time being. Curriculum development is now the process of responding to constant and accelerating change. The commitment is thus to the process of development rather than particular products.

Another traditional assumption which continues to inhibit progress towards a more participatory management process is the view that teachers have of their own work. Succeeding generations of teachers continue to mould themselves on the image of the instructor, the formal vehicle through which traditional wisdom and knowledge are dispensed to the young. This has encouraged the view that teaching is about performing, about acting a part and fulfilling a role. The view that what a teacher teaches is what a pupil learns is hard to dislodge, and great importance is attached to techniques of control and persuasion. Our increasing understanding that learning is a capacity of the learner rather than a function of the teacher has been hard to get across to teachers in general. The support given by the Plowden Report (Central Advisory Council for Education 1967) to this idea of teaching as a facilitation of the natural learning potential of the pupil continues un- heeded, as HMI have recently pointed out in their compilation of published reports of primary schools. This view of teaching as a performing activity is reinforced by the teacher-assessing activities of tutors, heads, Advisers and HMI (Gray and Coulson 1982). The introduction of a system of teacher assessment as currently envisaged by the government will strengthen this tendency even more. Later (Chapter 7) we propose forms of self-assessment for teachers and schools which are more in keeping with the notion of teachers as professionals.

In such circumstances it is understandable that teachers have become sensitive to comments about their teaching, even from their colleagues. Inevitably, curriculum development has become an activity to identify the content of teaching programmes. Considerations of classroom method and teaching style, because of their sensitivity, are left out, being regarded as matters of personal concern only to the individual teachers themselves. One of the reasons why curriculum development in primary schools has been so unsuccessful in recent years is that it has become largely a paper exercise – the preparation of guidelines and subject policies. How they are interpreted in practical terms in the classroom has been left to the discretion of the teacher. In the face of perceived threats from outside, schools and teachers have not been slow to develop a rhetoric of curriculum development.

Professional development also is severely hampered by this performance view of teaching. If professional competence and expertise are to be exten- ded there needs to be a climate in which the intensely practical aspects of classroom work are seen as an essential part of any curriculum-development activity. This will not be achieved if teachers, like the pupils they work with, day by day, constantly see themselves as being judged and graded. A judgmental climate is not an easy one in which to talk freely and openly about 'how' and 'why' you teach as you do, or indeed to identify areas where you may need help and guidance. Many teachers have learnt to hide away their professional inadequacies and pretend that they do not exist.

The power of traditional orthodoxy is clearly demonstrated by the fact that although there is as yet no national prescription for the curriculum, schools in Great Britain are characterized more by their similarities than their differences. Virtually all primary schools subscribe to the same half-dozen subject areas, devoting similar amounts of time to the pursuit of each. This somewhat monolithic approach to the organization of learning is perhaps explained by distinguishing the different sources of the received wisdom which perpetuates the system. These can be considered in terms of:

1. Precepts: the 'musts' of the schooling system.
2. Expectations: the 'oughts' and 'shoulds'.
3. Situations: 'the way we do things here'.

These three sets of factors operate on schools and teachers to sustain established practices. They have combined to develop a belief that the schooling system needs to be solidly uniform throughout, allowing little scope for individuality or variation. Change continues to be problematical because schools, unlike manufacturing enterprises, have not had to adapt to survive. Their continued existence is assured.

It is against this background of traditional assumptions that we must consider how professional roles and responsibilities in schools can help to create the adaptability that the future will increasingly demand. A new management paradigm is needed which will generate new assumptions, create new possibilities and establish new practices. Foremost among these new assumptions will need to be:

1. An appreciation that teaching, like learning, is about creating a human environment in which it is safe to reach out and take risks; in which not getting things quite right the first time is regarded as a good way to learn and to discover.
2. A realization that change is a constant and ever present feature of our lives, and that we do our pupils a disservice by sustaining a belief in the virtue of traditional orthodoxy.
3. A view of teaching as an activity of facilitation and not performance. A process of working alongside pupils in classrooms and finding, through the quality of our relationship with them, ever new ways to help them realize their amazing and ever present potential.
4. An understanding that management is an interactive process, a way of working together to achieve agreed aims through group cohesion rather than through attention to hierarchical separation and status differentials.

Leadership

Central to a new paradigm for school management must be a clear understanding of the part that leadership plays in creating conditions in which teamwork and cooperation are of a high order. In *Effective Leadership*, John Adair (1983) has suggested that leadership is related to the needs that arise within the organization – in our case the school. The practice of leadership involves an understanding of three particular sets of needs which are constantly interacting:

1. The needs of the tasks to be undertaken.
2. The needs of the staff team as a whole.
3. The needs of individuals within the staff team.

The role of the leader becomes one of adopting attitudes and behaviours designed to:

1. Achieve the task.
2. Build and maintain the staff team.
3. Develop each individual.

Current models of school leadership place far too much emphasis on the tasks as identified by the head and too little on the second and third sets of needs. Relating this threefold model of leadership to headship in a primary school we have:

1. Setting up structures to achieve the tasks identified and agreed upon by the staff.
2. Creating conditions and setting up structures for effective teamwork.
3. Responding to the needs of individual members of staff in terms of:
   (a) Their own personal and professional growth.
   (b) Their capacity to work and contribute to the team as a whole.

In this model, leadership needs to be seen more in terms of what leaders do, rather than who the leaders are and the positions they occupy in the staffing structure. Leadership, like management, is judged by results rather than intentions. This places the emphasis on behaviour rather than on plans and policies. Leadership needs to be conceived in terms of function of the staff team and not as a responsibility of a named individual. Effective teamwork is successful when there is a capacity in the group to allow the leadership to emerge in response to the need of the moment. When the group regards a single individual as 'the leader' then teamwork can become inhibited, constrained by expectations which relate to status and position rather than need and function.

Certain key qualities in teachers are closely related to successful learning in pupils. These same qualities are likely to contribute most to effective team work and group cohesion. Thinking now of leadership these can be defined as:

1. The ability to be a good listener and readily understand the world as perceived by colleagues.
2. The capacity to feel a warm, caring respect for each colleague as a unique and individual person.
3. The ability to engage in a genuine person-to-person relationship with each colleague and to be yourself in those relationships.

This, then, says something about how we need to behave in relation to our colleagues if we are to exercise effective leadership. The relationship of these qualities to the self-concept is considered in detail in Chapter 3. An awareness of the factors which contribute to a strong self-concept is necessary if roles and responsibilities are to be exercised effectively. They are (Elliott-Kemp 1982):

Self-awareness   The extent to which we are conscious of our own attitudes and values and of the effect our behaviour has on others.

Will to achieve   The extent to which we seek new challenges in our work and personal lives.

Optimism   The extent to which we feel positive about the future and our part in it.

Positive regard   The extent to which we respond to others with warmth, caring and respect.

Trust   The extent to which we are prepared to place trust in those with whom we work.

Congruence   The extent to which we are secure enough to be ourselves with our colleagues.

Empathy   The extent to which we are able to understand the circumstances of our colleagues' lives from their point of view.

Courage   The extent to which we are prepared to take risks in finding more effective ways of working with colleagues and the extent to which we are prepared to admit to a need for help from them.
(Extract printed by kind permissoin of PAVIC Publications, Sheffield City Polytechnic)

When these qualities are well developed in the individual members of a working group then teamwork is likely to be of a high order. Initiatives from any member of staff will be welcomed and status differentials will tend not to get in the way of the team's capacity to solve problems and achieve its tasks.

In moving towards group-focused management there will need to be considerable changes in the ways that we conceive and exercise roles and responsibilities. Leadership needs to be seen as a function of the group rather than a position, and more concerned with behaviour than with status. Such a transformation in attitude and practice will not be easy to accomplish. Progress needs to be made first by trying to develop accepted patterns and seeking more imaginative uses for existing structures. Let us look now at ways in which the present scale-post structure can be employed more productively.

The first model, the functional approach, represents an attempt to respond to the question: If there is a school plan, what tasks do we need to undertake?

The second model, the developmental approach, has a different question: If there is a school plan, how do we need to be?

The first approach responds in terms of tasks and activities. The developmental approach is concerned with the professional skills and qualities that the plan demands.

The functional approach

In this approach the structuring of scale posts is related to the management tasks and activities to be engaged on during a school year. These would include:

1. Curriculum development programmes.

2. Organizational changes.
3. Financial planning and review.
4. Staff development and INSET.
5. Policy-making.
6. Policy review.
7. Events in school calendar.

The approach builds on the assumption that scale-post-holders are best conceived of as co-managers of the school's affairs. The management tasks considered are those which are outside the daily classroom work of the teachers and which have implications for the work of the school as a whole.

In traditional scale-post structures the roles of individuals tend to have been created with no end point in mind. A role is occupied until such time as the teacher vacates the post. In the functional approach being proposed here posts are brought into existence to deal with a discrete and finite set of objectives. On their completion the post is reviewed and redefined. Once in operation a structure such as this becomes a dynamic part of the school's management process, supporting its current needs and planned policies.

Changing from a more traditional structure requires a careful approach and the cooperation of all teachers concerned. The transition is best preceded by some form of school appraisal which focuses on curriculum, organization, staff development, decision-making and staff participation. Such an exercise is often associated with the work of a newly appointed head and involves a comprehensive review of the work of the school (Whitaker 1983). A less complex approach would resemble the staff appraisal exercise described in Chapter 3. Its purpose there is related to the process of selection. Here it is concerned with the present management needs of the school.

This 'management review exercise' assumes an annual planning exercise towards the end of each academic year, the purpose of which is to define precisely how and when specific policies are to be carried out during the next academic year. Figure 2.1 proposes a way of breaking these policies down into discrete activities and events. The left-hand column suggests that policies have three particular dimensions – innovation, maintenance and review. These categories can be further subdivided if required.

The matrix (Figure 2.1) can be drawn on to a large sheet of paper and pinned to the staffroom wall. Brainstorming in small groups of three or four will generate a range of activities which can be transferred to the large sheet. Whole-staff discussion can then follow and agreement be sought on the

	Curriculum	Organization	Staff development	Events
Innovation				
Maintenance				
Review				

Figure 2.1 Management review exercise

activities to feature in the allocation of posts.

The next stage is to translate these responses into the discrete tasks to be carried out during the year. Before allocating them to individuals it is important to relate them to a timescale. This is best carried out by locating activities on a year planner. In Figure 2.2, two symbols are used to distinguish between activities which are process-based – occurring over time – and events. The circle indicates the starting point of a process, with the arrow point suggesting the planned completion time. The square indicates events. Coloured stickers are a useful alternative to drawn symbols. By way of example three particular activities have been entered on the year planner.

Task 1

This is a whole-school project entitled 'Growth' which will occupy the spring term. Although the culmination of the project will be an exhibition at the regional Science Fair the project is rooted in the school's policy for topic work. Associated with the work are three key events – two whole-day study visits either side of the spring halfterm, and the exhibition in the local town hall.

	Task 1	Task 2	Task 3
Autumn term		○ ▼ □ □	
	□	□ □	□
Spring term	○ ▼ □		○ ▼
	□	□ □	□ □
Summer term	□	▼	

Figure 2.2 Task planning exercise

This project is a major feature of the school's annual plan and will involve all teachers and pupils. The management tasks associated with it will be considerable and it is likely that all scale-post-holders will have some responsibility for it in their job outline.

Task 2

This refers to the innovation of a new approach to drama. A classroom has become available which is to be set up as an expressive arts studio. The plan, covering most of the academic year, involves a programme of in-service training. The events indicated are those occasions when the Adviser will be visiting the school to work with pupils and teachers in the new studio.

This is an important innovatory programme. The planning for it occupied a great deal of staff time during the preceding academic year. A small team of three teachers – one infant, one lower junior and one upper junior – was responsible for the development of the drama curriculum document; the deputy head and another teacher worked with the Adviser on the plans for the alterations to the vacant room; and the head working with the three remaining teachers designed the in-service programme. A successful introduction of this new curriculum programme will require considerable teamwork and create a wide variety of tasks and activities. All staff will need to have some element of this programme reflected in their scale post.

Task 3

These are the events associated with decision-making on the allocation of the school's capitation allowance. Detailed work will involve the deputy head and two other teachers. These are tasks which are rotated annually between the staff.

Following the allocation of all the tasks to the year planner comes the process of dividing up responsibilities. A cohesive team will be able to handle this as a whole-staff exercise, making decisions based on an awareness of the needs of individual teachers and those of the school as a whole. It is important to achieve both equity and balance in the composition of posts while at the same time achieving optimum conditions for success in the policies defined. Linking the scale-post structure to the school's staff-development policy should ensure that each post-holder has the opportunity to:

1. Utilize specialist skills and abilities.
2. Follow particular interests and enthusiasms.
3. Acquire and develop new skills and abilities.
4. Widen experience.
5. Accept new challenges.

Another set of considerations to apply are those of the various management functions. Each post-holder should have some opportunity for:

1. Planning.
2. Creating.
3. Communicating.

4. Motivating.
5. Organizing.
6. Evaluating.

If each of these functions is incorporated into the post then the opportunity to exercise leadership is likely to be a positive feature of the work. While it is important to achieve some spread of functions within each post this should not be gained at the expense of individual expertise. In the examples quoted above the good planners and motivators should be involved in the overall implementation of policies and programmes and the good organizers in the arrangement of events. In order to provide a satisfactory balance between utilizing existing skills and acquiring new ones it is useful to conceive of each post as having three distinct elements:

1. Involvement in a main project.
2. Responsibility for a key event.
3. A range of supporting activities.

This provides each post-holder with the opportunity to exercise overall leadership for a particular project, to act in support of other projects and to organize a key event. Not only would such a range of responsibilities contribute to the successful management of the school, the work would provide many fruitful professional development opportunities.

When activities have been allocated and each scale-post-holder has a clear brief it is vital to ensure that roles and responsibilities are accurately defined and documented. Each scale-post-holder should prepare a job outline containing the following:

1. Job title, e.g. 'Project Leader – Drama'.
2. A statement of objectives.
3. Key dates:
    (a) Project deadlines.
    (b) Project events.
    (c) Project meetings.
4. List of project groups and committees involved in.
5. Outline of how the post is to be conducted.
6. Requests to colleagues:
    (a) How you would like them to help you.
    (b) How you would like to help them.

All the job outlines should be prepared to a standard format and distributed to all members of staff, including clerical, welfare and technical colleagues. The success of any scale-post structure depends on everyone knowing in sufficient detail what each other person is planning to do, how they intend to do it and where responsibilities join or overlap. Role conflict can be avoided if this stage is well conducted and if the documentation is clear and comprehensive.

While it is good management and leadership practice for the head and the deputy to take a share of the tasks generated and to undertake project responsibility, it is also vital for them to have a coordinating and evaluating role. These essential functions can be facilitated by bringing into existence two key committees or working groups: the Policy Group, which deals with the main aspects of project design; and the Ways and Means Group, which is concerned with issues of implementation. In a small school where subdivision is not possible, it is useful to distinguish between these two distinct functions – the form of the policies and the detail of their practical implementation.

A further essential leadership function for the head and the deputy is to facilitate regular, at least half-termly, progress discussions with each scale-post-holder. Such discussions should be concerned with:

1. Assessing progress towards planned objectives.
2. Identifying and considering problems.
3. Clarifying future plans.
4. Evaluating outcomes.

Reviewing progress should also feature regularly in staff meetings, with time allocated for each post-holder to share current issues and concerns. In addition to this essential face-to-face communicating, it is important to establish an efficient system of information sharing. A specific noticeboard in the school office or staffroom should be set aside for the management programme. It should be subdivided, with headings such as REMINDERS, REQUESTS, NEXT WEEK and URGENT. This latter category should only be used sparingly and items should not be allowed to remain beyond the deadline to which they refer. It is also a good idea to use brightly coloured papers for notices under this heading.

The essential feature of the functional approach to scale-post responsibility is the annual plan. Since posts relate to the implementation of this plan it is important to consider how planning for the next academic year takes place. This can be both an on-going process, in that future needs are regularly featured in staff meetings, and a particular event in the management calendar. The Policy Group can be responsible for preparing a discussion document relating to the next annual plan, and the Ways and Means Group can take charge of the process of translating this into practical terms through activities described in this section. It is a good idea to keep the last half of the summer term clear for these activities.

Developmental approach

In this approach the emphasis is changed from one of attention to tasks and activities that need to be carried out to one of relating roles and responsibilities to professional growth and development. Like the first approach this one also assumes a clearly formulated programme for school development over a period of time, with its necessary year plans broken down into convenient term plans and more detailed action programmes. The key feature of this developmental approach is the linking of responsibility to the staff-development needs that are created by the nature of the agreed school plan.

Essentially the developmental approach provides an opportunity for a school to focus on the relationship of the teachers' classroom behaviour to the learning process. Unlike a great deal of curriculum-development work its main concern is not the nature of the learning programmes but how they are carried out in the classroom. Using the six management functions referred to in the previous section the key areas of focus will be:

Planning
1. The content and design of learning programmes.
2. Individual, group and class tasks.
3. The design of the classroom.
4. Working practices and procedures.
5. Monitoring and evaluation procedures.

Creating
1. New approaches to curriculum design.
2. New ideas for classroom organization.
3. Developing teaching styles.
4. Finding ways to involve pupils in classroom management.
5. Trying out new techniques.

Communicating
1. Building personal relationships with pupils.
2. Making time for listening to pupils.
3. Developing groupwork.
4. Developing relationships with colleagues.
5. Contributing to honest and open discussion.

Motivating
1. Understanding pupil behaviour.
2. Building an encouraging classroom climate.
3. Helping pupils to understand the learning process.
4. Relating learning to pupil interests and experience.
5. Helping pupils achieve a sense of belonging.

Organizing
1. Creating and maintaining a stimulating learning environment.
2. Organizing learning activities.
3. Implementing curriculum programmes.
4. Dealing with tasks and activities.
5. Working with colleagues and contributing to school management.

Evaluating
1. Comparing outcomes with plans.
2. Monitoring individual progress.
3. Matching work to ability.
4. Checking continuity and progression.
5. Evaluating policy programmes.

This is a selective list and by no means raises all the issues of classroom teaching. Any subset of this list would make a very useful agenda for a progress interview between head and scale-post-holder.

   In considering the professional development needs of a staff it is important to bear in mind the points made in the earlier section which conceived of leadership as a function of the group as a whole and suggested the following dimensions:

1. The task.
2. The group.
3. The individual.

This provides a useful way of relating roles and responsibilities to professional development. The task represents the desirable future the staff are working to realize. It will exist in the form of clearly defined aims and objectives and the corresponding programmes for achieving them. The programmes will call upon both the collective efforts of the staff working as a team and the individual contributions of each teacher. It is necessary, therefore, that role definitions refer to both group and individual needs. A practical way of raising an agenda for staff development is suggested in Figure 2.3.

Each member of staff should be provided with one form (as shown in Figure 2.3) for each project currently present in the school development plan. The aim is to invite each teacher to list his or her own particular needs in relation to that programme, categorized under the headings 'knowledge', 'skills' and 'qualities'. They are also invited to suggest what skills and activities will be necessary to achieve the sort of cohesive group process so necessary to effective progress.

When each member of staff has completed a sheet for each of the policy programmes it is necessary to define a role plan. This approach to responsibility focuses very much on the learning process inside the classroom and the teachers' particular skills and abilities. Each role plan is an attempt to provide a clear set of aims for professional development. Part of the

Project	Group needs	Individual needs		
		Knowledge	Skills	Qualities
Teaching				
Planning				
Creating				
Communicating				
Organizing				
Evaluating				
Leading				

Figure 2.3   Identifying professional development needs

headteacher's leadership role is to work with each member of staff to prepare a realistic but challenging role plan. This is best achieved through a series of one-to-one discussions.

The identification of the collective needs of the staff should be a team exercise. Much will depend on the capacities within the working group for frank and honest exchanges about how the group operates and what its strengths and its weaknesses are. The staff appraisal exercise described in Chapter 3 is a very useful activity to help bring out these issues. Developments in humanistic psychology and human-relations training during recent years have provided numerous insights into group processes and practice. Few members of staff are likely to have had the opportunity to be involved in the increasing number of in-service courses which focus on this aspect of management but it is important that part of the whole-staff commitment is towards increasing knowledge about group management and developing the skills that it requires.

When individual consultations have been completed and group needs agreed, it is important for each member of staff to commit his or her role plan to paper and to share it with colleagues. Part of the co-managing process is supporting colleagues in their endeavours, and it is essential that each teacher is clearly aware of the development programmes of colleagues. The role plan shown in Figure 2.4 is offered by way of example.

Since the emphasis in this approach is on the teachers' understanding of the learning process and the development of practical skills and abilities it is important that the operating procedures of the scheme provide opportunities for regular review and appraisal. Since appraisal interviews are a time-consuming activity for one person to handle, a system of peer-group appraisal is recommended. This requires each member of staff to work with a colleague to review progress and consider problems. About once a month each pair of teachers agrees to meet for an hour and a half or so. Each partner should complete a form as shown in Figure 2.5 at the beginning of the meeting.

Following the completion of the questionnaires one partner listens while the other talks through the issues raised on the form. The role of the listener is to help the talker to clarify issues, to identify problems and to seek explanations and solutions. The listening role is essentially a helping one, of assisting the talker to be clear about the work under review. It is not an opportunity for giving advice but for enabling the other to deal with the issues under consideration. After half an hour the pair swap roles for the next half-hour. The final twenty minutes of the session should be devoted to

Name:	Term ending:
Professional development objectives	
1. Personal – working alone	
Intention	Outcome
1. To attend course on group-focused learning 2. Follow up ideas in the classroom 3. Attend drama workshops 4. Work on Open University pack – *Curriculum in Action* 5. Continue studying Cockroft Report	
2. Group – working with others	
Intention	Outcome
1. Join drama project team 2. Attend course for staff – 'Developing active listening' 3. Try out peer-group appraisal interview with colleague 4. Contribute to policy-group meetings 5. Run a staff workshop – 'Group-Focused Learning'	

Figure 2.4   Role plan

generating and sharing new objectives which will be reviewed next time. The final task is to fix a date, about a month ahead, when the outcome of this session can be considered. This particular approach to peer-group appraisal benefits if participants have received some training in active listening, or basic counselling skills. Opportunities for such training are increasingly available within LEAs, through Adult Education Centres and from agencies specializing in such training.

Name:	Date:	
What I had planned to do	What happened	What I still have to do

Figure 2.5   Role-plan analysis

In practice

Two distinct approaches to the identification of roles and responsibilities have been presented in this chapter. The purpose of offering different models has been to pinpoint the alternative approaches to the traditional ones. In practice some combination of the two approaches described here is to be desired so that teachers in their co-managing capacities are concerned both with the tasks and activities of development policies and with the extension of their own personal and professional skills. The choice of model is itself an interesting and essential whole-staff exercise. Moving from a long-established pattern to a new one can be a difficult process (see Chapter 5). However, if the exercise is approached as one of the staff team's projects for the year then there is an opportunity for all avenues to be explored, and there is ample time for both group and individual needs to be brought out into the open for discussion and consideration.

Whichever approach is chosen, the structuring of roles and responsibilities is a key management task for the headteacher. The structure is more likely to be successful if it helps to satisfy the motivational needs that were referred to earlier in the chapter. Teacher behaviour will supply plenty of information about how these needs are being met, but in progress interviews with each member of staff the head needs to be listening for clear evidence in each of four key areas (discussed in more detail in Chapter 4):

Affiliation
1. To what extent does each member of staff feel a strong sense of identity with the school, its policies and philosophy?
2. In what ways does this sense of belonging express itself?

Achievement
1. To what extent does each member of staff feel a real sense of achievement about his or her contribution to school life?
2. In what ways does this sense of achievement express itself?

Appreciation
1. To what extent does each member of staff feel valued and appreciated for what he or she brings to the school?
2. In what ways does this sense of appreciation express itself?

Influence
1. To what extent does each member of staff feel he or she is influencing the course of school events and developments?
2. In what ways does this sense of influence express itself?

In practice the aim should be to create roles and responsibilities that are rooted in the daily lives of teachers. In this way they are more likely to make optimum use of the range of skills and capabilities present in the working team. The essential departure from past practice must be in developing the idea that responsibilities are a key feature of an effective management partnership. It is through the exercising of this partnership in corporate planning and decision-making that progress can be achieved. A well-planned and coordinated role structure can facilitate this process of co-managing and help to create the dynamic flexibility necessary to ensure that policies and programmes are responses to the changing needs of society and its young learners. All this presupposes an efficient and effective selection process which will ensure as far as possible that roles and responsibilites are perceived clearly by the staff and are of relevance and use to individual and institutional development.

References

Adair, J. (1983) *Effective Leadership*, London: Pan Books

Central Advisory Council for Education (England) (1967) *Children and Their Primary Schools* (The Plowden Report) vol.1, London: HMSO.

Department of Education and Science (1975) Report of the Committee of Inquiry appointed by the Secretary of State for Education and Science under the chairmanship of Sir Alan (now Lord) Bullock. *A Language for Life*, London: HMSO.

Department of Education and Science (1978) *Primary Education in England: A Survey by HM Inspectors of Schools*, London: HMSO.

Department of Education and Science (1982) Report of the Committee of Inquiry into the Teaching of Mathematics in Schools under the Chairmanship of Dr W.H. Cockcroft. *Mathamatics Counts*, London: HMSO.

Elliott-Kemp, J. and Rogers, C. (1982) *The Effective Teacher*, Sheffield: Sheffield City Polytechnic.

Gray, H. and Coulson, A.A. (1982) Teacher Education, Management and the Facilitation of Change, *Educational Change and Development* vol. 4, no. 1.

Whitaker, P. (1983) *The Primary Head*, London: Heinemann Educational Books.

CHAPTER 3

THE SELECTION OF STAFF

Having considered the roles and tasks of leadership, and the ways in which the curriculum may be enhanced through shared considerations of priorities and decision-taking, we now move on to the all-important process of recruitment and selection. In times of increasingly stable staffs this management task becomes ever more critical, and this chapter offers practical suggestions for: systematically appraising the needs of the school; establishing criteria for selection; providing appropriate information for candidates; eliciting relevant information from them about their experience, abilities, interests and expertise; supplying and obtaining reports; interviewing and induction.

It is unfortunate that the period of falling rolls in primary schools has coincided with a national economic crisis. In a more enabling financial climate falling rolls would have offered a unique opportunity to expand and improve the quality of primary education. The sad reality is that primary education over recent years has suffered badly, not because of falling rolls themselves but because local authorities have been under pressure to rationalize on staffing and to restrict the movement of teachers. Ring fences have grown around local authorities to such an extent in primary education that it can now be easier to get a headship in another LEA than a permanent scale 1 post.

The result of the twin pressures of falling roles and shrinking resources is a change in the pattern of recruitment. Not only has the balance of supply and demand altered, but the changes in the rules and regulations relating to appointments have also had considerable implications for the mobility of the teaching force. For the head and governors of an individual primary school this has meant a sometimes drastic reduction in the power and opportunity to make appointments of their own choice. Redeployment, even when handled creatively and with sensitivity by local authorities, has created a new pattern of appointing. Because the key issue has tended to be the adjustment of staff sizes to a reduced number on roll, the teachers moving between schools have not necessarily been those who would have chosen mobility. Teachers with an eye to career development have avoided sideways moves only to find later that such moves become necessary in order to buy wider experience. Open and unrestricted advertisements for teaching staff are increasingly uncommon below the headship level. The nature and practice of staff selection and appointment is now somewhat different from what it was five years ago.

It is against this background that we must consider how a restricted selection process can best be managed to provide the optimum control for head and governors. This chapter will attempt to offer insights into the organizational implications when teaching vacancies arise within a school and to provide practical suggestions for managing the process of recruitment and selection. The procedural aspects of recruitment and selection have been dealt with in some detail elsewhere (Whitaker 1983). This chapter will consider some of the less well-defined aspects of the process.

Since procedures differ considerably between local authorities it is not possible to take account of individual variations in approach and practice. In practice, the process is managed through a partnership between the governors, the headteacher and the local-authority administration. For the purposes of writing we have assumed that the local-authority administration determines the procedures that shall be followed but that the headteacher and the governors manage the selection process. Since this book is about the professional management of the school our main concern is with the part played by the head and other members of the staff in the selection process.

A vacancy becomes available

The necessity to make an appointment to the teaching staff is a major management opportunity for the headteacher. The departure of a valued colleague will create a sense of loss, both in the sense that valuable expertise will be lost but also because a significant element of the school's social cohesiveness will be removed. It can be difficult to envisage life in a school without one of its key contributors. Perhaps this is because we tend to be preoccupied more with the task elements of management – the structure of the school, the nature of the curriculum and the professional qualities of teachers – than with the human relationships. There are conceptual models of school organizations and curriculum guidelines in abundance but very little which actually helps to inform about the behavioural dynamics of school life and the way they contribute to the overall effectiveness of the school as a working environment for learning.

In contemplating a replacement for a colleague it is very tempting to allow a dream to temper reality. How nice it would be in one simple appointment to plug all the gaps, satisfy all the needs and accelerate the journey to the promised land. Much of headship is about coping with the gap between the image and the reality, and once the fantasizing is over it is necessary to address the very real question of how the vacancy should be filled.

It is important at this stage to establish who will be involved in the various procedures of the selection process. This has implications for the leadership style of the head and the extent to which individual teachers and the staff as a whole are involved in the overall process of managing the school. In Chapter 1, leadership was described in terms of the providing of an environment. It is very much in this way that we see the context for the process of selection. One of the key themes of this book is the necessity for staff to be involved as active participants in the total managing process of the school. Given such a model of the management process, the needs of the individual are the needs of the organization. Decisions are going to be made about the professional effectiveness of the school and about the nature of the staff as a working team. If the selection process is to be successful in satisfying needs then clearly it is vital for staff to be involved. The head has the initiating and coordinating functions and carries responsibility in final decision-making, but needs to work very closely with colleagues throughout the whole process.

Assessing the needs

The assessment of needs is an exercise to determine the current perceptions of the staff about how the school is currently working. Specifically it provides an opportunity to review:

1. Where we are hoping to go.
2. Where we have come from.
3. Where we are at the moment.

This in turn requires consideration of:

1. What we are currently engaged on.
2. What we need to do next.

Before considering what sort of person to appoint it is necessary to be reminded of the work currently in progress and of the plans due for implementation in the future. The idea will be to try and appoint someone who has a positive contribution to make in these specific directions. The head is in an ideal position to summarize the progress made in implementing plans but it is important to gather staff perceptions as well. Raising the five issues listed above can help to provide a clear picture of current work and future tasks. The details provided by schools to potential applicants for posts rarely, if ever, give an indication of the current state of a development programme. This is unfortunate because it robs the candidate of an opportunity to make the written application specifically relevant to current issues and concerns.

In addition to the developmental aspects of the school there are also the general professional requirements which need consideration. Merely holding a generalized image of 'a good teacher' in the mind is unlikely to be very helpful. In giving attention to professional qualities it is necessary to be clear and specific. Figure 3.1 suggests the sort of checklist that can be

Categories	Knowledge	Skills	Qualities
Teaching			
Planning			
Creating			
Communicating			
Motivating			
Organizing			
Evaluating			
Leading			

Figure 3.1   Professional qualities checklist

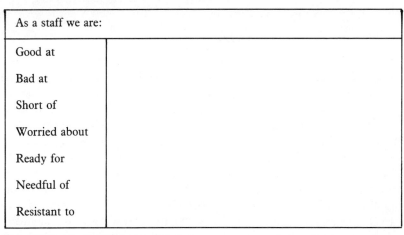

As a staff we are:	
Good at	
Bad at	
Short of	
Worried about	
Ready for	
Needful of	
Resistant to	

Figure 3.2　Staff appraisal exercise

generated to help in this analysis. The categories listed down the left-hand side allocate spaces for teaching, managing and leadership elements to be identified. It is useful to subdivide these into knowledge, skills and qualities. Such a check-sheet should form part of a school's staff-development procedures and can be used by teachers as a self-appraisal instrument. It becomes especially useful in trying to identify the general and specific requirements for a vacant post.

Staff appraisal exercise

A useful strategy for involving the staff in this assessment of needs is the following staff appraisal exercise. The focus here is the staff as a team, rather than its constituent members, and the needs that arise from their corporate activities. The exercise can be handled in various ways. A reasonably cohesive staff will be able to manage it in an open staff meeting, spending a few minutes brainstorming responses to each category. If the staff is large it is best to subdivide into smaller groups of four or five. The brainstormed responses should be listed and displayed for further consideration and discussion. An alternative approach is to have response sheets printed as illustrated in Figure 3.2. These can be made available to staff to fill in at their convenience. A compilation of responses can be made for circulation or display.

The categories listed are merely suggestions. Staff should be encouraged to create their own categories or delete ones they do not feel are helpful.

Choice of categories and avoidance of particular ones can also provide an interesting insight into the current psychological health of the staff.

Having established an idea of the professional qualities required in the vacant post and produced an assessment of the current attitudes and perceptions of the staff as a whole it is necessary to consider the type of personality that is likely to match the needs identified.

Personality and behaviour are much more powerful factors in selection than is sometimes realized. Time and again, in our experience, it is personal considerations that prevail in the making of a final choice from candidates shortlisted for interview. Heads and governors are always anxious to appoint someone who is going to 'fit in'. This implies that there is already an appreciation of how personal factors interact within the school. When heads make this statement about 'fitting in', do they mean someone who fits their ideas of a suitable person, or someone who will blend with the staff and enhance social cohesion? Much will depend upon the way that the head relates both to individual members of staff on a person-to-person basis, and to the working team as a whole. No staff is fully cohesive, and interpersonal and intergroup conflict is a feature of all social groups.

In schools where corporate leadership and participatory management are of a high order there is a capacity to deal with conflict in an open and creative way. In these circumstances staff see conflicts as issues to be resolved rather than matters to be settled in terms of winning or losing. Such teamwork is more likely to be achieved where staff members have strong and well-developed self-concepts. Teachers with a high self-concept have been shown to be more effective in facilitating successful learning in pupils than those with a low self-concept (Rogers 1983). Effective teamwork is more likely in groups where members have well-developed self-concepts. In summarizing the research into personal qualities and teaching, Carl Rogers (1983) has suggested that in the process of staff selection we should be searching for those teachers who:

1. Have the ability to be good listeners and can most readily understand the world as perceived by the pupil.
2. Tend to feel a warm caring and respect for each pupil as a unique person.
3. Are secure enough to be themselves with their pupils, who are not seen as roles but as real persons.
4. Tend to believe that persons are, at core, constructive not evil.

These qualities related to the self-concept are not always the ones that we tend to look for in our recruiting. It is not enough to follow hunches about personality (although the intuitive response to people does have distinct value). It is important to try and check out these qualities in those we consider for our vacancies. How we do this will be discussed later in the chapter.

Assessing needs is a crucial part of the selection process. In schools where there is a policy of continuous self-appraisal it need not occupy much time or energy. What is important is that the assessing is looked at from various points of view: the needs of the pupils; the needs of individual teachers; and the needs of the staff as a whole. The intention should be to generate a realistic but comprehensive category of personal and professional attributes necessary for the job in hand. Without this it will not be possible to match the potential skills and qualities of the applicants to the needs of the school.

Before proceeding to the next stage of the selection process it is important to consider whether as a result of the vacancy arising some internal staff adjustments are necessary or desirable. Having identified current needs consideration should be given to whether the potential to satisfy some of them already lies within the staff. The departure of the school's main musician, for example, could provide an opportunity for another musical member of staff to come forward. Some teachers live in the shadow of more experienced and qualified colleagues and allow their talents to become subdued and under-utilized. When considering specialist needs the first option should always be to give existing members of staff the opportunity to adjust their responsibilities. The departure of a key teacher can be an internal motivator, presenting other members of staff with the opportunity to move into new areas and take on new challenges.

Providing information for candidates

The education service has something of a bad reputation in the area of the provision of information for candidates. Potential applicants are expected to consider a major upheaval in their working circumstances on the barest of information about the job being offered, and sometimes when applicants seek an opportunity to visit a school where a vacancy exists they are received only grudgingly. The whole system of appointing staff seems to be built on the wrong assumption. Some schools and local authorities give applicants the impression that they are doing teachers a favour by offering up teaching posts for application. The opposite is true. A teaching vacancy in a school is a staffing problem which only those willing to leave their present employment can solve. Those with the power to appoint should be much more grateful than they often appear that teachers are prepared to put themselves out to satisfy these staffing needs. While costs are a major consideration they should not be used as an excuse for discourtesy. It is quite appalling that some teachers, having spent considerable time and care in preparing applications in response to advertisements, receive no letters of acknowledgement or even a note regretting that on this occasion they have not been successful.

Cost is the main reason used to explain why advertising for teaching posts is so inadequate. All that an advertisement can be these days is an indication that a teaching post is available at a particular school and that more detailed information can be obtained on request. This part of the appointing exercise – the provision of the further details – is vitally important and should be approached with a determination to provide interested teachers with as clear a picture as possible of the school, and of the teaching vacancy that has arisen within it.

The first purpose that these details serve is to limit the number of applicants. There can be no justification for putting anyone to the time and expense of applying for a post for which they are unqualified or for which they do not satisfy the basic criteria. The aim must be positively to attract those candidates who do satisfy the identified requirements and to inhibit those whose applications will not receive serious consideration. From the details the candidate should be able to gain a clear appreciation of the job involved, the type of school, something of the values encouraged in the school and an indication of the experience and professional qualities hoped for in the successful candidate.

It is not easy to summarize these requirements so as to satisfy all the anticipated queries by interested applicants. All schools should have a document which provides a great deal of the information – the school brochure, which is made available to parents. While this has been written with a parent audience in mind it should contain a great deal of the information which applicants will need. Clearly, then, this should be one document that is made available. What the brochure will not contain is any specific information about the post available. It is the nature of this information that we must now consider.

A useful exercise, and one that is vastly improved if the whole staff are involved in it, is that of putting yourself in the position of an interested applicant and listing all the queries you are likely to have. This can be conducted in very much the same way as the task described in the previous section of this chapter. Sheets of paper with category headings can be provided and colleagues can be encouraged to brainstorm the sorts of questions they would have if they were in the position of applicant. The following list is offered by way of example:

Type of school
What sort of community does it serve?
How is it organized?
What specialist facilities does it have?
Is it open plan?
Do staff change year groups every year?
How are curriculum decisions made?
Is there a school policy on multicultural education?

Teaching role
In which age group is the vacancy?
What is the classroom like?
How many pupils?
What range of equipment and resources?
Are there policies about teaching style?
Are there curriculum guidelines?

Special responsibilities
Is there a job description?
To whom would I be accountable?
Are there funds available for development?
Is this a new or a replacement post?

Parents/community
Is there a school policy on community education?
Are parents active in the school?
Is there a PTA or parents association?
What is the neighbourhood like?

Professional support
Are there regular staff meetings?
Is there a staff-development policy?
Do the staff have the opportunity of regular appraisal interviews?
Is there school based in-service work?
Are staff involved in policy-making?

This is by no means a complete list but one that provides a useful agenda for preparing documents that supply candidates with information about, and insights into, the life and working of the school.

The next stage is to prepare documentation. How the documentation is presented will convey a great deal about the value system of the school. Shoddy and badly produced papers suggesting that the school prides itself on high standards raises the question about self-awareness. Information prepared in the first person, either singular or plural, always has a more personal quality about it and also serves to initiate a written conversation to which the candidate can respond in the letter of application. One of the best ways to approach the task is for someone to take the list of brainstormed questions and attempt to draft a few paragraphs for each category. Other colleagues can be invited to add information that may have been omitted. There is a lot to be said for this drafting being undertaken by a teacher on the same professional scale as the vacant post. Not only is this good management and healthy delegation, but from the applicant's point of view it is perhaps more informative to get a colleague's view of the situation rather than the head's. The head will of course have other information to supply, particularly in relation to the requirements of the post and an indication of the skills and qualities being sought.

Finally in this section it is important to consider the information which is provided to candidates about the application itself. Generally the nature, style and composition of the written application is left for candidates to decide. Most teaching posts from scale 1 to headship are applied for in the same generalized way of completed application form and a supporting letter. Written applications could become a much more profound and effective part of the selection procedure if steps were taken to encourage candidates to address themselves to the specific issues of the post under consideration, rather than the generalized matters of concern to the profession as a whole. One step towards this end is the preparation for potential candidates of guidelines for completing the application. By specifying the issues for consideration in the application form we are ensuring that what candidates write relates to the post in hand and not to a wider range of general and sometimes not particularly relevant material. The aim should be to get the candidate to prepare an application form which gives the selection panel the maximum amount of relevant information on which to base their judgments. It may be a good idea to issue candidates with a supplementary question sheet designed to elicit particular information not covered by the application form – the question sheet shown in Figure 3.3 is offered as an example.

Please suggest a few strategies for improving staff involvement in curriculum development	
Please comment on your reactions to *Education Observed* published by the DES in December 1984	
How do you suggest topic work can be improved as a central element in the primary curriculum?	
Which particular aspect of in-service training has been of help in preparing you for this post?	
What opportunities for professional development do you see in this post?	
What would you regard as the single most significant contribution you have made to your present school?	

Figure 3.3   Question sheet for candidates

The specimen letter shown in Figure 3.4 is provided as a summary of the main points of this section.

Visits and visiting

It is becoming increasingly common for teachers to want to visit schools before committing themselves to a formal application for a post. This is a very sensible preliminary step for the teacher and an opportunity for the school. The visit of the potential candidate serves two very important functions. First, it provides an opportunity for the candidate to gain insights into the school and the way that it works. Second, it provides an opportunity for the head and the staff to meet a potential colleague.

Nothing less than a half-day in a school is likely to be adequate to satisfy the candidate's needs. In arranging the visit the head and staff need to be aware of its fundamental purpose – to create conditions in which the match of person to post, and post to person, can be assessed. In the expectation that a number of candidates will accept the invitation to visit it is necessary

Dear Ms Smith

Thank you for your enquiry about the vacant scale 2 post at this school. I enclose the following information which I hope you will find helpful in giving you an idea of the school and how we go about things:

1. A copy of the school brochure.
2. A staff handbook.
3. A job outline.
4. Some information about the school compiled by the staff.
5. Some notes about the skills and qualities we are hoping for in the successful candidate.

I also enclose the application papers. If, after having looked at the documents you decide to apply I shall be most grateful if you will submit the application in the following way:

Application form
Please complete pages 1, 2 and 3, leaving the back page blank.

Question sheet
These questions, as you will appreciate, relate specifically to the post you have enquired about. Please write your responses in the spaces provided.

Supporting letter
In a supporting letter of about 1500 words I shall be grateful if you would include some reference to your ideas on the following ideas:

1. The role of the scale-post-holder in the modern primary school.
2. Relationships with pupils.
3. Learning from first-hand experience.

We are hoping to hold interviews in the first week after halfterm and invitations will be sent out two weeks before that. In the meantime if you would like to visit the school we shall be very happy to receive you. Please telephone the school and we will try and arrange a mutually convenient time.

Yours sincerely

Figure 3.4 Specimen letter to enquirers

to have agreed a procedure for managing the visit. The following checklist suggests the different elements of a visit:

1. Seeing the building, inside and out.
2. Visiting classrooms and talking to pupils.
3. Noting specialist facilities: resources, library etc.
4. Meeting staff informally.
5. Interview with headteacher.

In organizing such a visit it is important to consider who should do the conducted tour of the school. This is probably better handled by a member of staff other than the head. It is good for the visitor to get another teacher's view of the school and it is likely to be easier for the visitor to raise issues which might be difficult if the head were conducting the tour. In order to allow some space and time for the visitor to get a 'feel' of the school it is good to keep the tour reasonably short and then to invite the visitor to wander. This allows the candidate an opportunity just to absorb what is going on, to think out possibilities, to anticipate experiences, to sense the organizational dynamics and to reflect on impressions. Motivation will be a key considertion, and will be based on the answers to such implicit questions as, 'Am I encouraged by what I see here?' and 'Is this school likely to develop me and help me grow, both personally and professionally?'

The discussion with the headteacher is really an interview conducted by the candidate. It is his or her opportunity to have the head's view on a range of issues about the running of the school and the new teacher's part in the scheme of things. Sometimes the head will wish other colleagues to be present at this discussion since some detailed questions might be better answered by the deputy, year coordinator or curriculum consultant.

The head and staff also have a great deal to learn from the visit of a potential colleague. In the discussion the head will gain an insight into the teacher's attitudes and values simply from the questions that he or she asks. The teacher's personal behaviour around the school will have been noticed, in terms both of relationships with pupils and of reactions to what is going on. Interpersonal behaviour will be a key consideration in attempting to assess how well the person 'fits' in relation to the staff as a whole. In fact from the moment the visitor sets foot in the school the inferential system of communication will have been at work and a great deal of evidence will be accumulated about the teacher and his or her particular personal and professional qualities.

Since there may be quite a time gap between the visits of interested teachers and the final selection interviews it is important that the impressions gathered about visitors are documented. A typed summary should be prepared which can be used in the final selection process alongside other confidential reports and references.

Some controversy surrounds the issue of heads visiting potential candidates in their schools. This is an important issue about which there needs to be general agreement in the profession. At present some heads visit before shortlisting; some only visit candidates they have already decided to call for interview; and some heads do not visit at all. This can be confusing for applicants and a code of practice would help to eliminate some of the suspicion that surrounds the issue. Our own view is that in an activity as practical as teaching a complete assessment of a candidate's abilities cannot be achieved without some opportunity to see him or her at work. On the other hand a satisfactory assessment is difficult to achieve from a very short visit, a glance at the classroom display and a brief chat with the teacher about what the pupils are doing.

If the headteacher is considering visiting candidates, the first consideration is when to do it. Should the visits be for the purpose of informing the shortlisting process, or of gaining more information about candidates already selected for interview? Only the first of these seems to make any sense. If it is the teacher's practical abilities which are the main consideration then visits should be undertaken to ascertain which have the abilities required. A large number of applicants may present a problem and it may be necessary to draw up a list of the candidates who on paper come closest to satisfying the requirements of the job.

If visits are intended it would be sensible to suggest this in the details sent to candidates. Certainly they should be told of an intended visit and some time should be made available so that the candidate can explain to the visiting head some of the situational factors about the school – catchment area, school building, resources and organization. The circumstances of the visit can provide the basis of very interesting and relevant questions if the candidate is later called for an interview, for example: 'I noticed when I visited your classroom that a number of pupils were undertaking individual assignments. Could you explain to us how that system works?' The answer to such questions should provide a number of opportunities to probe the issue of classroom organization and management in some depth.

When visiting teachers, the head should be very clear about the purposes of the visit. A schedule of factors should be drawn up and applied to each visit. Impressions and supporting evidence should be documented and a summary prepared for presentation at the shortlisting and perhaps again at the final interview. At some stage, perhaps at the end of the visit, the candidate should be asked how far he or she felt that what was seen was a typical representation of the class at work. It is essential that the head should take full account of the context within which the teacher is working and the extent to which the teacher's work is conditioned by school policies and practices.

References and confidential reports

A reference or confidential report is a formal way of conveying information from someone who knows a candidate to someone who is seeking to fill a vacant post. It is unfortunate that the whole business of seeking and supplying confidential reports is plagued by so much spurious protocol. Far too often reports are merely bland versions of telephone conversations that have already taken place. Heads telephone other heads to gain information in order to shortlist and then seek confirmation of that report in writing if the candidate is shortlisted for interview. When they are actually read out in the final stages of the selection process they usually only confirm views that have already been arrived at. It is rare to find that a confidential report has supplied information that is crucial to the selection process itself.

The fault lies essentially with those who are seeking the report. If specific information is not asked for then it is unlikely to be supplied, and what will be produced is a general appraisal that is characterized by excessive use of superlatives, or couched in the jargon of euphemism. What enquirers often do seek is an indication whether the candidate justifies an unreserved recommendation – a sort of five-year guarantee of good service. Not only is this a naive request, since it suggests that there is such a thing as all-purpose professional perfection, but it demeans the whole process of professional appraisal and evaluation. What should be asked for is an assessment of those skills and qualities in the candidate which specifically relate to the job under consideration.

There are a number of ways to obtain this information. Let us first of all be clear about the points about which the referee needs to be briefed before he or she can give a useful reference. This briefing involves:

1. Providing for the referee a clear written outline of the job in hand.
2. Identifying those particular skills and qualities which are hoped for in the successful candidate.

Dear Mr James

Ms J. Smith has applied for a scale 2 post at this school and has given you as a referee. For your information I enclose a copy of all the information which was sent to candidates. I hope this will serve to inform you about the job Ms Smith is being considered for and to give you an idea of the particular qualities we are hoping for in the successful candidate.

I also enclose a question sheet which seeks your comments on specific aspects of Ms Smith's work. Attached to this is an assessment sheet. I shall be most grateful for your responses to the questions and for your evaluation. I shall also be most grateful for any other information you may wish to draw to our attention.

As you may know we are hoping to hold interviews in the first week after halfterm. We shall be shortlisting at the end of this month and would very much like to receive your comments by then.

Many thanks for your help.
Yours sincerely

Figure 3.5   Letter to referee

3. Suggesting to the referee the criteria for the assessing of those skills and qualities.
4. Enabling the referee to have an opportunity to represent the candidate on issues not specifically referred to.

The specimen letter in Figure 3.5 suggests a possible approach. This letter makes reference to two further documents. The question sheet (Figure 3.6) seeks to gain specific information about the applicant's professional abilities. The assessment sheet (Figure 3.7) invites the referee to make a judgment about specific skills and qualities. Used in combination these two documents can provide a far more detailed and helpful appraisal of the candidate than the four or five paragraphs of general summary usually supplied.

Interviewing

An interview is a structured interaction between one person and another, or between one person and a panel. Those conducting the interview have the

What are the applicant's particular skills in building a classroom climate conducive to effective learning?	
What are the applicant's particular skills in classroom organization and management?	
What do you consider have been the applicant's most significant contributions in his/her present post?	
Which particular qualities in the applicant would you consider to be especially relevant to the post under consideration?	
What particular contribution has the applicant made to life in the staffroom and to staff discussion?	
Which of the applicant's personal qualities have contributed most to the school?	

Figure 3.6   Referee's question sheet

power to control the interaction, deciding how to conduct it, what material to deal with and when to end it. The interviewee acts in a responsive way to initiatives taken by the interviewers. It is important to be aware of this, and to have a capacity to see the experience from the candidate's point of view. Because of its formality and the fact that promotion may depend on it, an interview is usually quite a nerve-wracking affair. It is not a very common experience for most of us, and demands a somewhat unnatural style of behaviour. Also, an elaborate mythology has grown up about the unwritten rules of interviews – the way to dress and how to respond to the panel. Those conducting the interview bear considerable responsibility for helping the interviewee to cope with the situation and to be sufficiently at ease to provide the information the panel will need if it is to do its work well. It should always be the aim of an interviewing panel to enable candidates to perform at their best.

During the course of the interview and in the decision-making that follows it a number of skills are utilized:

1. Questioning.

Please indicate your assessment of the applicant's qualities by drawing a ring round one of the numbers in each category.

1: Excellent
2: Very good
3: Good
4: Adequate
5: Less than adequate

Creating an effective classroom learning environment	1	2	3	4	5
Planning work	1	2	3	4	5
Building relationships with pupils	1	2	3	4	5
Matching work to the ability of pupils	1	2	3	4	5
Working with colleagues	1	2	3	4	5
Motivating pupils	1	2	3	4	5
Relationships with parents	1	2	3	4	5
Energy and commitment	1	2	3	4	5
Evaluating and monitoring work	1	2	3	4	5
Responding to and developing new ideas	1	2	3	4	5
Flexibility of approach	1	2	3	4	5
Ability to seek help and support	1	2	3	4	5
Awareness of own strengths and weaknesses	1	2	3	4	5

Figure 3.7   Applicant assessment sheet

2. Listening.
3. Observing.
4. Summarizing.
5. Assessing.

Let us look at each of these in turn.

Questioning

This includes all those strategies designed to get the candidate talking. There is always a danger that those interviewing will do far more of the talking than they should, thereby failing to draw from the candidate sufficient data on which to base an informed judgment.

Questions are really invitations for the candidate to talk. Sometimes the best way to facilitate this is not to ask questions at all but to define an area upon which you would like the candidate's comments. For example, on the issue of classroom organization a possible question could be: 'What factors do you need to take account of when setting up a classroom for a class of first-year juniors?'

There are a number of limitations to this question. First, it generalizes the issue, asking the candidate to comment on what teachers in general might regard as significant factors in classroom organization. Second, it invites a somewhat superficial response since situational factors will be of the essence – the size of the classroom, the previous experience of the pupils, the preferred teaching style of the school and the educational philosophy prevailing within it. Third, it limits the candidate to theoretical issues rather than practical ones. Perhaps a better way to get the candidate talking on this issue would be: 'Would you like to tell us about the process you go through at the beginning of each academic year when you prepare the classroom for your new class?'

This 'open' question has a number of advantages. First, since it is not a 'closed' question designed to elicit specific, predetermined information, it does not presuppose a single correct answer. Second, it draws upon the most significant aspect of the candidate's capacity to do the job – his or her practical classroom experience. Third, it provides an opportunity for the interviewer to match the candidate's perception of an issue with information already obtained from other sources – the visit of the head to the candidate's classroom and the specific information about classroom organization received in the confidential report. An important consideration in the interview process is the extent to which the candidate's perceptions of his or her work matches that of others.

In preparing themselves for selection interviews candidates are often preoccupied by the questions they may be asked rather than the areas they may be invited to comment upon. This emphasizes one of the myths about selection – that success depends on getting the answers to the questions right. Such a view misunderstands the nature of the professional examination which a selection interview should be. Far more is of interest in the interview than simply the answers. Candidates need to be helped to the view that the interview is concerned more with what they have learned from their experience and with their particular skills and qualities than with mere knowledge. For this reason it is important that invitations to talk are not merely questions requiring a simple factual answer. Obviously some factual data may need to be established during the interview and some closed questions may be necessary, but the bulk of the interview should be concerned with drawing out from the candidate the more profound aspects of professional ability and potential.

Let us be clear about what we are trying to discover or confirm in the candidate. Basically it is information about:

1. The candidate's knowledge about, and understanding of, the process of education.
2. The candidate's practical skills and qualities.
3. The candidate's attitudes and values.

There is a relationship between the phrasing of questions and the category of information elicited:

1. 'What' questions usually elicit factual information.
2. 'How' questions usually elicit practical information.
3. 'Why' questions usually elicit attitudes and values.

There is a tendency in candidates to respond to questions with what they are most comfortable with, rather than with the information that has been asked for. Interviewers need to be on the watch for this inclination to answer a different question. When probed about attitudes and values, candidates will sometimes try and avoid that issue by offering an example from practical experience. A supplementary question is vital if the panel is to obtain a comprehensive understanding of the candidate's ability – far too often the candidate's answer is accepted and the questioning moved on to another issue or another member of the panel. It is much more profitable to stay on an issue and probe deeper into it, using the candidate's first answer as the cue for a more penetrating enquiry. When, for example, the candidate has offered a 'what' answer to a 'why' question, it is important to press the point and seek out the 'why'.

Earlier in the chapter the importance of the self-concept was stressed. Since quality of teaching relates closely to the factors contributing to the self-concept, it is important to cover these factors in the interview. Even without asking specific questions about these factors, the nature of the candidate's self-concept should be revealed during the interview. A check-list of the factors would be a useful addition to the headteacher's interview documents, perhaps arranged as in Figure 3.8, with spaces to record particular instances of each characteristic.

In preparing for the interview the panel need to play around with the phrasing of questions, being very clear about what it is they are hoping to find out. Badly worded questions are unlikely to bring the best out of a

Self-awareness	
Will to achieve	
Optimism	
Positive regard	
Trust	
Congruence	
Empathy	
Courage	

Figure 3.8   Self-concept factors

candidate, and a complicated preamble to a question is only likely to cause confusion. The best policy is to be very clear about what it is that you are wanting to discover, and then put the point to the candidate as simply as possible, following it up with precise supplementaries where necessary.

Listening

The ability to listen effectively in the interview is of fundamental importance. Far from consisting merely of hearing what is said, listening is the active and dynamic process of attempting to gain insights into the perceptual, intellectual and emotional world of the candidate. This involves a capacity to relate the candidate's responses to the questions posed and to pick out the distinguishing features of the candidate's presentation. In terms of the three categories already referred to this means being able to distinguish between answers which provide factual information, those which indicate skills and qualities, and those which reveal attitudes and values.

In the interview, listening operates at at least two levels. First, there is listening to make sense out of the current response – the immediate question. Second, there is listening to see how this answer relates to others that have come before or that will follow later. This is listening for consistency – the extent to which the candidate reveals a cohesive and compatible pattern of theory and practice. This second level of listening

Name:				
Appearance	Facial expression	Eye contact	Voice	Gestures
Knowledge				
Skills and qualities				
Attitudes and values				
Specific points		General comments		

Figure 3.9 Interview recording sheet

requires a capacity to pick out the underlying themes in the candidate's package of responses, in particular prejudices, ambiguities and inconsistencies.

Note-taking is a vital aid to effective listening in the selection interview. Since the process of interviewing itself requires considerable concentration it is important that data is recorded so that it can be recalled during the decision-making process. Figure 3.9 suggests a form that can be used by panel members to jot down significant points arising from each candidate's interview. A standard format makes for clarity and consistency between the panel members.

Observing

This is the skill of drawing inferences from the candidate's behaviour during the interview. Most interviewers can detect signs of nervousness in a candidate – a somewhat stiff posture, fidgety hands, a shaky voice – but may not be so aware of other aspects of non-verbal behaviour. Since the candidate's behaviour is likely to make an impression on each member of the interviewing panel it is important to make it an explicit feature of the selection process. During the summing up and decision-making process it is essential that these aspects of the candidate are dealt with openly, rather than left only as private impressions. The purpose of observing how people behave is to gain an understanding of why they behave as they do. The categories of non-verbal behaviour of significance in the interview will be:

1. Facial expression.
2. Eye contact.
3. Voice.
4. Gestures.

In combination these represent the candidate's 'presenting image'. There is a considerable literature on non-verbal communication and it is important that someone on the interviewing panel has some knowledge and skill in this area. (Chapter 4 goes into this subject in some detail.) There is always a danger that incorrect interpretations will be drawn and this is another reason why some discussion of this dimension is important.

Perhaps the most significant aspect of the 'presenting image' is that of dress. There is much talk of 'the interview suit' and whether women candidates should wear trousers to an interview. There are many prejudices relating to this aspect, which is why the issue of appearance should feature in the discussion. In these times of changing fashions and social codes it would be good to see an initiative being taken by selectors, suggesting that candidates should attend interview in the style of clothing they would normally adopt in the classroom.

Summarizing

From time to time during the interview it is helpful to summarize progress. This provides an opportunity to check out with the candidate ground that has been covered and also that the candidate's view has been correctly received. In addition it provides an opportunity for the interviewing panel to assess its own progress. It is during the final decision-making discussion that the skill of summarizing is most important. It is important, when reviewing the interviews of each candidate, to be able to bring in front of the panel a complete appraisal of the candidate's strengths and weaknesses as revealed by the interview. This view will need to be supplemented later with information and assessments from visits and confidential reports.

To present such a summary requires some sort of framework. A summary could be built on the interview recording sheet illustrated in Figure 3.9. Alternatively the summary could be arranged under a set of categories decided upon before the interview:

1. Ability to deal with the interview.
2. Interview behaviour and 'presenting image'.
3. Professional knowledge and understanding.
4. Skills and qualities.
5. Attitudes and values.
6. Relationship of abilities to job requirements.
7. Estimation of potential to do the job.

Wherever possible the panel should be encouraged to adopt a standard procedure for summarizing and assessing each candidate. Far too often the final selection procedure rests on the exchange of personal impressions unrelated to the requirements of the job under consideration. Such an approach can be achieved if the panel includes a representative of the LEA's central administration, either an Adviser or an Officer.

Assessing

This is the skill of drawing conclusions from the evidence obtained about each candidate. This part of the procedure is facilitated considerably if the summarizing described above has been of a high order. In working towards the final choice of candidate it is important to proceed by elimination – no candidate should be eliminated without some discussion. If the procedures before the interview were carried out effectively all the candidates called should have the potential to do the job well. Some may not interview as well as others and the skill of assessment is about distinguishing between interview expertise and wider professional ability. It is at this stage that it is necessary to remind the panel of those particular abilities and aptitudes hoped for in the successful candidate and also the important personal qualities that need to accompany them. The following checklist suggests the factors that need to be included in the assessment that precedes the final choice of candidate:

1. A restatement of the current and future needs of the school.
2. A restatement of the job requirements.
3. A restatement of the skills and qualities hoped for.
4. Summaries of the interviews of each candidate.
5. Discussion of each candidate's interview.
6. Presentation of information previously received from:
   (a) Visits of candidates to the school
   (b) Visits to the candidates in their schools.
   (c) Confidential reports and references.

If the last item has been dealt with by a presentation before the interviews then it will be necessary to go over some of the main points concerning each candidate. Part of the assessment is the process of comparing the first-hand evidence of each candidate in the interview with reports received from other sources. It is not enough to make a choice purely on the basis of the interview itself. The interview stands as a part of a comprehensive selection process and needs to be seen in the context of that wider perspective.

Most interviews for teaching seem to last between twenty and forty minutes. If the interview, as perceived in this chapter, is to succeed in becoming a more effective instrument in the process of staff selection it is necessary to plan for interviews that are somewhat longer. This will provide an opportunity for more supplementary questioning, a chance to go into some issues in greater depth, and more scope for exploring the range of a candidate's qualities and abilities.

Induction

Once an appointment has been made there is a tendency to regard the selection process as complete. In a sense the interview itself could be regarded as the beginning of that often neglected process – the induction programme. This officially comes into operation the moment a post has been offered and accepted. Although the successful candidate will have to serve out time in an existing post there is much that can be done to prepare for the new job ahead.

Before leaving the school after the successful interview the candidate may well have the opportunity to meet future colleagues and to make some arrangements to visit before officially taking up the post. This would also be a good time to pass to the candidate such documents as curriculum guidelines, pupil profiles, minutes of staff meetings and recent newsletters to parents.

A comprehensive induction programme should be an essential ingredient in a school's staff-development policy. Some care should be taken to anticipate the needs of a colleague joining the staff, and key members of staff should be briefed to undertake important introductory activities. Far too often new members of staff are left to tease out for themselves those all-important behavioural rituals and customs such as terminology, use of first names, and procedures for administrating the school's bureaucracy. Certainly the induction of a new colleague should be the subject of at least one staff meeting.

The relationship between staff development and staff selection is fundamental. As has already been stated, those schools which have well-established staff-development practices will see selection as a natural part of that process. The need to appoint a new member of staff also provides a creative opportunity to exercise staff development by involving the whole of the professional team in the process of selection. Such an involvement has the potential to build effective teamwork and strengthen the social cohesiveness which is at the heart of all effective management. Indeed, both the newest and the longest-serving members of staff have a right to continuing opportunities for developing their awareness and expertise as individuals and as members of a team.

References

D.E.S. (1984) Education Observed, a review of published reports on primary schools, by H.M. Inspectors, Middlesex: DES Publications, Department of Education and Science.

Elliott-Kemp, J. and Rogers, C. (1982) The Effective Teacher, Sheffield: Sheffield City Polytechnic.

Gray, H. and Coulson, A.A. (1982) Teacher Education, Management and the Facilitation of Change, Educational Change and Development vol. 4, no. 1.

Rogers, C. (1983) Freedom to Learn for the 80s, Columbus, Ohio: Charles E. Merrill Publishing Company.

Whitaker, P. (1983) The Primary Head, London: Heinemann Educational Books.

CHAPTER 4

DEVELOPING PROFESSIONAL AWARENESS AND EXPERTISE

It is not enough to have a stable staff. Without help and encouragement in tackling not only new issues caused by external interventions but also the day-to-day challenges and problems caused by virtue of being a member of a teaching and learning community, many teachers will 'die on the vine', become disenchanted, or settle into a routine which may ultimately become dysfunctional. It is therefore important that the head ensures that opportunities for updating skills and knowledge are provided on an individual and collective level, and that the psychological health of the school is maintained. This chapter provides both useful ideas for further thought and practical suggestions for action by the head in, for example, staff meetings and staff appraisal.

The term 'staff development' is used a great deal these days and sometimes it seems to be interpreted as an activity which happens at specific times during each school year or a teacher's career. What it ought to be is an on-going process which is taking place every day in the school, and one whereby the head, through leading the teachers in a professional manner, ensures that they are well informed and fully aware of their roles, and the responsibilities which they have to the head, their colleagues and the children they teach. One of the most satisfying aspects of the head's job is the growth of personnel under his or her supervision. It is important, therefore, that the head has given very careful consideration to the management of a personal leadership style in order to get the best out of the staff and develop their potential. Consequently the head will need to reflect on how to communicate with staff, establish priorities, manage the time available, delegate responsibility and motivate the staff. Without frequent thought on these issues he or she is unlikely to develop the teachers' professional awareness and expertise, and the teachers are, after all, the most important resource available within the school.

Keeping everyone informed

How can ideas be communicated to others effectively? This is a question which every head should ask when preparing for staff meetings or parents' evenings, or talking to individual members of staff. Just because the head is familiar with the topic to be talked about does not mean that the teachers or the children's parents are. As schools grow in size and complexity there is a temptation for the head to rely heavily on formal written statements to spell out policy and philosophy, although experience suggests that written statements may not be the most effective method of getting ideas across. There are other ways of communicating within schools which are more likely to unify the school and project a positive image and outlook.

The head must become the catalyst for keeping information flowing throughout the school. Everyone involved in the life of the school – pupils, teachers, other staff, parents and governors – must be informed about those policies and practices which affect their lives. Teachers are unlikely to be highly motivated when they read about new approaches to the organization or curriculum of the school in a letter to parents. Parents want to be informed about changes in organization before they take place, while governors will be more than frustrated if the head acts on all matters without consultation. It is the head's role to make certain that every school group has some input in making decisions and carrying out mutually agreed goals and objectives.

Timing is a key factor in keeping everyone informed, and when change is planned it can be worth while to list all the people who may initially be affected by it. Everyone should be informed *before* the change becomes effective and it is essential that they have had the opportunity to air questions and comments at an early stage and in an informal atmosphere where communication can move freely. Statements of school policy seldom run foul when there is free access of staff members to the head. Ideally, all the staff members will be part of the policy-making team. People who feel that they have been an integral part of a policy decision then have a vested interest in seeing that it succeeds. The teacher who is merely told of a change via a written memo is likely to become disgruntled and feel left out. (See Chapter 5 for a full consideration of possible effects of innovation and change on teachers.)

Keeping people informed is more than telling them in a pleasant manner. They must understand the reasons for the change. Alternatives should be presented. Suggestions must be considered and objections should be studied. The final decisions should take into account the feelings of every group. Gone are the days when the head maintained an 'I know best' attitude and imposed his or her will on docile teachers, obedient pupils, and awestruck parents.

Systems of communication

Every head wants good staff morale and this is largely dependent on the effectiveness of the systems of communication. In most cases the two main means of communication used will be written communications and face-to-face meetings. The latter must always predominate and the most obvious way is to get around the school during the day. Visiting every classroom every day should be the first priority so that staff have access to the head of the teaching team, who in turn can use such opportunities to communicate philosophy and influence classroom practice. In some rooms it may be a cursory visit, while in others it may be long enough to participate in a discussion or assist with children's activities. Teachers and pupils must know that the head takes an interest in them in their place of work. They should not see the head solely behind a desk in an office. It is important that the staff see the head when they arrive in the morning and, however the head may be feeling, a cheerful word of welcome will usually not go amiss. Seeing the teachers at the end of the day is probably more important because it is a good time for a head to compliment a teacher for something outstanding observed when making the rounds of classrooms. Offering praise to a teacher when other staff members are within earshot can be an effective motivator, but if there is a desire to make suggestions for improvements then this should always be done in private.

Staff meetings

These are an essential ingredient in the development of effective communications as they offer an opportunity for everyone to share ideas. It is important to remember that the staff have not come to a meeting just to listen to the head's magnetic voice, and any announcements the head needs to make should be kept brief, as people cannot sustain interest for long periods of time. Staff meetings must be planned well in advance – generally at least a term ahead – so that staff know what their commitment is likely to be. This is particularly important if the meetings are taking place after school, in which case a specific time should be fixed for the meetings to start and finish. All the staff must fully understand the purpose of such meetings and an agenda should be drawn up which includes all topics of interest suggested by individual teachers. A written agenda should either be given to each staff member or placed on the staff noticeboard at least 24 hours before the meeting is due to take place so that everyone has time to think about their own contribution on the topics raised for discussion.

An opportunity should be offered at the start of the meeting for staff to add items, and an effort should be made to establish initially the priorities and order of business. The agenda should not be sacrosanct, however, and if more important issues emerge during the meeting, which members are keen to pursue, then agreement should be sought to postpone the rest. The purpose of the meeting should always be clear, whether it be decision- or policy-making, exchanging information or keeping in touch. The chairperson's role is to help the group to achieve its task of completing the agenda whilst helping the members to work with each other effectively. It is good practice to allow the deputy head and those with special-responsibility posts to chair specific meetings, especially when a curriculum area which relates to a teacher's specific responsibility is under discussion. Keeping a record of decisions reached is also an important aspect of staff meetings which is sometimes overlooked and this task can be delegated to staff members in turn with the notes of each meeting subsequently displayed on the staff-room noticeboard for perusal at leisure.

In order to make meetings work effectively the leader, in many cases the head, needs to give careful consideration to working with the participants before, during and after the meeting. The following reminders are a guide to the strategies which need to be employed:

Before the meeting
1. Consider the individuals involved and the interests they will bring to the meeting.
2. Consult with staff regarding the agenda and time of the meeting.
3. Provide any necessary information prior to the meeting.
4. Organize tea or coffee and ensure the room will be comfortable and appropriately laid out. Staff should be able to look at and talk to each other.

During the meeting

1. Ensure that it starts on time.
2. Establish contract related to the content, style and purpose of the meeting.
3. Check out the feelings and understanding of staff members as the agenda progresses.
4. Use humour appropriately.
5. Bring any latecomers up to date.
6. Convey in behaviour that members are respected and contributions to the meeting are valued.
7. Listen, encourage, respond, link, bring in, ask clarifying questions, support, offer feedback to members.
8. Check any domination and work for a balanced contribution amongst staff members.
9. Encourage the talking out of differences.
10. Thank those attending and observe the agreed time limits.

After the meeting

1. Follow up contact with individual teachers who may need a further chance to talk on matters arising from the meeting.
2. Check out the staff feelings about the meeting and whether there are any suggestions for making the next meeting even more efficient.
3. Support any agreed follow-up action undertaken by the staff.

The staff meeting is perhaps the most used and least effective medium in most schools. If it goes well, the gains, in improving communication, participation, commitment, and a sense of teamwork, are appreciable. If it does not, if issues are not clearly presented, if agendas are mismanaged or people left feeling confused, manipulated or frustrated, the individual and organizational costs can be appreciable.

Encouraging participation

There are a number of effective strategies which can be employed to increase staff participation in meetings. For example, when developing school-based in-service curriculum meetings:

1. The leaders of the development (which should include either the head or deputy head and, where appropriate, one other member of staff) must

define their roles: they must see themselves as learners, refrain from 'selling' ideas, and allow staff to elaborate those ideas they see as relevant to the needs of the school.

2. Two team leaders are of great help in the planning stage to ensure the application of a breadth of experience to the development of the programme. Their role is also to stimulate discussion of the work undertaken when each session is concluded.

3. Before the 'course' begins there must be a slow build-up to the first session, during which time staff are given the opportunity to become acquainted with the philosophy involved.

4. The involvement of teachers from other schools within a local area can broaden the discussion and prevent staff from becoming too inward-looking.

5. Group sizes for discussion should be kept to a minimum of three and a maximum of six – this results in greater teacher participation especially when careful consideration is given to the membership of each group.

6. In order to ensure full involvement by each staff member, it is desirable to appoint individuals on a rota basis to act as rapporteur to any plenary sessions.

Noticeboards in the staffroom are another effective way to communicate ideas and administrative details. Far too often such boards become cluttered with papers which are pinned at random in any available space and as a result lose the impact they were designed to have on the reader. Such a staff noticeboard should be clearly subdivided in sections so that staff know where to seek information. There should be sections on in-service courses, duty schedules, teacher union announcements etc, and a 'special' section should be reserved for items of immediate concern. All items should be neatly displayed, and stale, out-of-date notices should be removed promptly.

However, the more formal systems of communication are not the only ones operating in the school. A great deal of information is likely to be transmitted through both the informal system and the inferential system. The informal system, the 'grapevine', is certainly at work in any school and there is little that can be done to prevent it functioning. It clearly differs from the formal systems in that it tends to be quicker and less accurate, and to thrive on 'news' that threatens and alarms. The head needs to recognize that rumour and gossip are essential elements in the social psychology of any institution. To ignore such elements would be foolish, and the head needs at least to take them into account. The grapevine can have considerable impact if left to grow wildly.

Non-verbal communication

The inferential system consists largely of non-verbal communication, which by its very nature will always be present yet is often not given careful consideration. Non-verbal communication can be split into two categories, visual and non-visual, both of which are important in their own right. The different areas of visual non-verbal communication are as follows:

Proximity

How close (physically) you get to an individual will be taken as an indication of how close a relationship you have with him or her.

Orientation

The way you sit or stand in relation to someone is an indicator of the type of relationship you have with him or her. People will always try to face those with whom they are in conflict, or whom they are trying to prove superiority to, whereas people who are cooperative and friendly will either be side-by-side or at 90 degrees to each other.

Bodily posture

This will indicate your attitude towards someone as well as your self-image. It is easier for a leader to attain a relaxed position in a group if he or she sits or stands in the group norm position.

Gestures

There are two types of gestures – head nods, and other body movements such as hand or arm movements. A single nod is a method of showing attention when talking to someone, and a rapid series of nods usually shows that you wish to interrupt the speaker and get your own point of view across. The other type of gestures (other body movements) can be a great source of information, especially when spontaneous – they can show specific as well as general emotions.

Facial expression

People's expressions indicate their attitudes and emotions toward each other and situations. A smile may sometimes indicate happiness, interest or greeting: a frown can mean distaste or concentration. One of the problems with the interpretation of facial expressions is that they can be manipulated to give a false impression.

Eye movement

These can indicate attention as well as moving in synchrony with speech. The amount of eye contact with speakers can also indicate the degree of interest being shown in what people are saying.

Appearance

People's hair, clothes, make-up etc can indicate self-image, personality, mood, occupation. You decide how you wish to look and what others see may well determine their reaction to you.

When considering non-visual, non-verbal communication there tends to be a problem of perception. As so much information is taken in visually, it becomes difficult for people to perceive other types of non-visual information, especially if it contradicts the visual sense. There are four types of non-visual, non-verbal communication which can give information about people's feelings and attitudes:

Touch

It is remarkable how even such a formalized gesture as a handshake can convey an impression of someone's personality.

Aura

This is difficult to define but one's perception of it could be termed 'intuition'. People who are experiencing very strong emotions generate a strong aura which can be detected fairly easily by other people.

Voice

One of the best indicators of a person's feelings is the voice. The speed of speech, the tone of voice, the choice of words, and the loudness as well as hardness of the speech, can all indicate general and specific emotions.

Olfactory

A person's choice of perfume, aftershave etc can give an impression of self-image, personality, and mood.

Non-verbal communication is a powerful means of indicating attitudes and emotions and probably has two other main uses: first, re-enforcing, contradicting or complementing verbal communication; and second, replacing speech.

Keeping ideas flowing

Not every good idea originates in the head's office. Seeds of ideas are more often developed in the classroom, where the good head is constantly on the look-out for such ideas and innovations. It becomes the head's job to help these seeds germinate and to nurture their growth. He or she must also provide the atmosphere and structures in which teachers are willing to share ideas and pass on successful practices. The head should therefore encourage informal meetings between groups of teachers in order that an interactive flow of information and attitudes is stimulated. The technique requires little more than an openness which allows ideas to rise from the grass roots rather than percolate down from the head's office.

Heads have developed many ways of finding out what their teachers are thinking. They can range from interview techniques to simply leaving the office door open. Each listening device has its virtues and its limitations. While some are clearly better than others there is no single method which can give you all the information you need about teacher ideas and attitudes. The daily face-to-face communication with the staff is unquestionably a fruitful source of information about what is really going on in the school. Without these contacts no other method of listening is likely to be very meaningful.

Yet, no matter how free and open heads may try to be, staffs will always have a strong tendency to tell them what they think they want to hear. Communication is most likely to be 'taken on board' if it is personal and fulfils a need or meets an interest in the receiver. When the head spends time listening to individual teachers he or she will often be drawn into impromptu conversations. This is an ideal opportunity to develop a good working relationship with staff, and will not only give a close personal insight into their ideas about the school but provide an opportunity for the head to share thinking about the way the school and their work is developing. By responding to teachers' needs the head will be creating an atmosphere of trust and understanding. Every effort should be made to be clear and consistent in any replies, otherwise all the head may do is confuse the situation, and this may well lead to rumour and misunderstanding. There will be occasions when people will misunderstand him or her and on analysis it will probably be the case that it was the head who did not achieve the necessary degree of precision and lucidity in the first instance.

Active listening

A developed skill of active listening will be of great help in communicating effectively with other people. By active listening we mean the ability to see the expressed idea and attitude from the other person's point of view, to sense how it feels to him or her, and to achieve his or her frame of reference in regard to the topic being talked about. Active listening is the skill of feeding back to the sender the feelings which are perceived from his or her verbal and non-verbal communication. The goal of active listening is really to 'hear' what senders are communicating about their feelings through their verbal and non-verbal language; in other words hearing what is said accurately and interpreting what is not said. The skills of active listening will usually be a help to someone who is bothered by a professional or personal problem. In order to develop the skill there is a need to:

1. Concentrate – aurally and visually.
2. Clarify and help the discussion by:
   (a) Paraphrasing what has been said.
   (b) Summarizing at appropriate stages.
3. Hear the speaker out.
4. Respond to feelings and emotions – don't sweep them aside.
5. Respond to non-verbal cues.

Establishing priorities and procedures

Think carefully about your school – what are your goals or objectives for improving it? What steps have you taken this year to implement your plans? Have you only managed to maintain existing practices or are developments clearly recognizable? Some heads seem to have difficulty planning because they regard it as limited to 'thinking', whereas in fact it ought to be thought of as a writing exercise. In one way or another, whether you have been aware of it or not, you will have been thinking about the goals for your school. But thinking about your goals is quite different from writing them down. Unwritten goals often remain vague dreams. Writing goals down tends to make them more concrete and specific and helps you probe below the surface of the same old clichés you have been telling yourself for years.

By reading your thoughts committed to paper you will gain a valuable new perspective because you can then examine them more closely. Once they have an independent existence you can scrutinize them better – they can be analyzed, refined, updated, pondered and changed. At the same time write down the names of the people who could help you achieve some of the goals and in this way you will begin to realize specific ways that the skills and efforts of such people can be utilized.

Before the start of a new school year set yourself the task of writing three or four goals that you would like to accomplish during the year. Early in the autumn term meet with each of your staff members and talk with them about the year ahead. Ask them what some of their plans are and discuss them in detail. At the first convenient staff meeting after seeing each of your teachers, the goals for the school year should be discussed. However, long-term planning must be complemented by short-term planning. This kind of planning requires specifying the activities which teachers should perform. Most, if not all, of the activities specified in long-term plans, should contribute to the realization of the goal specified in long-term plans, and should be planned in such a way that they are recognized as achievable by your staff. To set them tasks which they feel are completely beyond them is pointless.

As head, it is vital that you examine the precise job that is to be performed by each of your staff involved. Each teacher will have a different set of experiences, attitudes and ideas and your role is to develop each of your staff to a level which utilizes their existing expertise, yet takes them one step further in the development of classroom practice. In writing specific objectives for your staff the following suggestions will help in your planning. An objective should:

1. Be mutually agreed.
2. Be recorded in writing.
3. Specify a single result to be accomplished.
4. Set a target date for its accomplishment.
5. Be measurable and verifiable.
6. Be realistic and attainable but still represent a challenge.

Establishing priorities with your staff and listing them is only part of the planning process. All the items on the list will not be of equal value so it is important to agree with your staff the ones which are of the highest priority. Having done this you will end up with a first priority which should be of very high value and which you need to build into your daily schedule. Teachers may need help in ordering their priorities for the year and it is your job to review their progress.

The effective management of time

Some teachers and heads can get vast amounts done during a working day while others continually complain that they do not have enough time. It seems that some people are able to use their time better than others; and heads who recognize planning as an important function of their role usually find themselves in the former category. Planning separates the effective head from the neurotic one, and in today's primary schools it is as important for the head to have knowledge and skill in implementing the management process – planning, organizing, directing and controlling time – as a knowledge of the curriculum. Planning is determining what needs to be done, who will do it, and when it has to be done.

The first step you need to take in effectively managing your own time is to find out how you spend it at present. A precise study is not necessary, but a time analysis chart (Figure 4.1) using a check mark for each ten minutes of each day, can give a fairly accurate picture of how most of your time is spent. The same sheet can be used for an entire week as this will have greater impact and be easier to check. The total check marks for the week in each column multiplied by ten provide a fairly accurate picture of how many minutes are spent in a week on each activity. (You will have to determine the column headings for yourself in order to choose those which best cover your own activities.) Once you have discovered how your time is spent you may well realize that it does not allow for any of your set priorities and this is where a personal planning sheet (Figure 4.2) can help you to organize your time for the coming week. It will force you to evaluate activities, set priorities, and schedule each activity when it will not be crowded out by a dozen others. During the week some tasks will not be completed, and so will need re-scheduling. Nevertheless, this kind of planning, where an explanation in writing is given to oneself for non-completion of tasks, will give you a better understanding of, and more control over, how your time is used.

Managing personal time in this way is obviously good in theory, but many heads back away when they look at the countless activities which they must

TIME	Teaching	Visiting classrooms	Paperwork	Telephoning	Informal meetings with individual teachers	Staff meetings	Parent consultations	Visitors – governors, Advisers, etc	Duties – dinner, playground	Visits to other establishments
08.00										
08.30										
09.00										
09.30										
10.00										
10.30										
11.00										
11.30										
12.00										
12.30										
13.00										
13.30										
14.00										
14.30										
15.00										
15.30										
16.00										
16.30										
17.00										
17.30										

Figure 4.1　Personal time analysis

Week commencing:											
Activity	Monday		Tuesday		Wednesday		Thursday		Friday		Comments
	a.m.	p.m.	a.m.	p.m.	a.m.	p.m.	a.m.	p.m.	a.m.	p.m.	

Figure 4.2   Personal planning sheet

engage in every day. Feeling that it is hopeless, they never start, and so put personal time planning far down on the mental list of things they will do as soon as they get more time. None of us is perfect. None of us should be disappointed if we are not planning our work – and working our plan – every minute of the day, but you will be taking several steps in the right direction if you get into the habit of doing the following:

1. Keep long-term goals in your mind even while doing the smallest task.
2. Plan first thing in the morning and set priorities for the day.
3. Keep a list of specific items to be done each day, arrange them in priority order, and then do your best to get the important ones done as soon as possible.
4. When under pressure, ask yourself, 'Would anything disastrous happen if I didn't know now?' If the answer is no, then don't do it.
5. Do your thinking on paper.
6. Set deadlines for yourself and your staff.
7. Delegate all routine items.
8. Generate as little paperwork as possible.
9. Recognize that some of your time will be spent on activities outside your control and don't worry about it.
10. Ask yourself hourly, 'Am I making the best use of my time right now?'

Managing teachers effectively

Communication is a two-way process and it is important from the head's point of view to be specific. Decisions, as well as the reasons for them, have to pass both ways before coordination and cooperation can be achieved.

Heads of schools should not hesitate to go into classrooms to find out what is going on. They should not have to pause and think twice before entering the classroom of one of their teachers. Only by frequent visiting will they be aware of the teachers' techniques, strengths and limitations. Only then will they be able to guide and provide true supervision by improving the level of instruction.

To manage teachers effectively, therefore, heads must resist any temptation to go into isolation. Teachers must see them in their classrooms and around the school – their 'aura' must pervade the entire school. By making their presence felt through communicating face-to-face they will begin to be truly effective in keeping their staffs informed. But they must not assume that teachers know everything that they know, or even that the teachers care about the same things as they do.

Teachers can be trained to improve their daily performance if they are approached in the right way. The best in-service programmes in the world may look good on paper but will be worth little if the wrong person is put in charge of implementing them. As leaders of the school heads must set an example of concern for self-improvement. They must show their teachers that they care about their feelings before they will be able to get the teachers to care about refining their techniques. The following suggestions are intended to help in the planning of a programme of school-based in-service training:

1. Make sure all your instructions are detailed and that you have anticipated any questions your staff may have.
2. Tell your staff the 'why' and 'what for' of any development.
3. Carefully describe the standards you expect.
4. Allow sufficient time for the completion of any task.
5. Plan for staff to visit each other's classrooms and other schools.
6. Demonstrate how you would like something taught.
7. Supervise closely.
8. Help the staff to set goals and objectives.
9. Be patient. Encourage with praise when earned.
10. Use staff expertise to encourage others.

11. Set the tone for self-improvement by being honest about your strengths and weaknesses.

In all his or her dealings with teachers and others in the school, the head needs to be ever protective of their egos and feelings of self-worth. This is perhaps the most important element in any programme of staff development. The head may be right about something, but if he or she presents correction in a manner that demeans the recipient, the latter will pay little or no attention to it. There will be times when the head must criticize, but it should always be done in a way that is constructive and not destructive. In addition, management of teachers will improve if the head remembers that positive feedback on the performance of teachers is also possible.

Feedback

Feedback is to help the receiver achieve the desired learning goals and objectives. It increases a person's awareness of how he or she affects others. Feedback is a mirror for observing the consequences of one's behaviour. Before giving feedback, a good relationship with the receiver needs to be established so that both parties can then be open and honest with each other. A good relationship will increase the chances of the feedback being accepted, not rejected, by the receiver. When giving feedback it is necessary to concentrate on:

1. What is done or said – not who said it or why. (i.e. do not make assumptions about motives or intent.)
2. Observations – not inferences (they may be wrong).
3. Description – not judgments or evaluations (which will be based on your own values).
4. 'Here and now' behaviour – not 'there and then' (which tends to become distorted or fantasy).
5. Sharing ideas and information, and explaining alternatives (rather than giving clearcut standard solutions).
6. Behaviour that can be reasonably changed (in order to avoid frustration or the rejection of the feedback).

Other factors you should consider are:

1. The value of feedback to the receiver – not your own self-satisfaction.
2. The desirability of limiting yourself to a few major observations to avoid

overloading the receiver.
3. The appropriate time and place to avoid emotionally harmful effects.

It may be helpful to check with other observers, before giving feedback, whether they have the same impression as yourself. It is also very important to check whether the receiver has understood and accepted the feedback by asking him or her to recap on what you have said. There is little point in giving feedback unless you are aware of any obstacles to the receiver accepting feedback. Some people find it hard to admit their weaknesses and difficulties, often because they are so concerned about what others think of them. They may fear being dependent on others or being without anyone upon whom they can depend for support and sympathy. Also they may feel that their problem is so unique that no one will understand, or equally that the problem is too trivial to bother anyone else with.

Reviewing teacher progress: the appraisal interview

Providing feedback is an activity which can happen at any appropriate time during the school year, but in addition to this there is probably a need for a more structured session when the head can review the progress and future objectives of each teacher. Such an appraisal interview or work review is an important part of motivating staff, improving performance and determining future developments. Some heads feel that because they are in daily contact with their staff there is no need for formal appraisal interviews. However, daily contact is often superficial and does not allow people time to discuss their ideas in depth. The appraisal interview can allow staff the time to consider their influence over the development of their skills and attitudes and, where appropriate, future promotional opportunities. The need for this type of interview has probably never been greater than in the present climate, where there is now more staff stability in primary schools – as a result of falling rolls – and consequently less rapid promotional opportunity, especially at scale 2 and 3 levels. For many teachers there is not the chance to move between schools to widen their experience. Therefore, every effort needs to be made to help teachers develop their expertise over a longer period within each school. The appraisal interview can assist both teacher and head in their personal and professional growth. A number of stages can be identified which lay a good foundation toward understanding and acceptance of the appraisal:

Stage 1: preparation

Prepare yourself, as well as asking the teacher to prepare him or herself, for a prearranged meeting at a mutually agreed time when there will be at least forty-five minutes available for an uninterrupted conversation. Come to the meeting expecting to compare notes, as this will allow for a review of the facts which have influenced the teacher's performance during the previous year.

Stage 2: review

Compare the teacher's accomplishments with specific targets. Do not be vague or resort to generalizations. Be specific about what was expected and how close the teacher has come to meeting those expectations.

Stage 3: giving praise

Be sure to give adequate credit for what has been accomplished. It is a temptation to concentrate on the mistakes and take for granted those things which have been done well.

Stage 4: noting areas for improvement

Review those things which have not been accomplished and emphasize where improvement is needed. Explore together with the teacher why improvements are necessary and how they can be tackled.

Stage 5: protecting the other's ego

Avoid the feeling of being judgmental. Never compare the teacher with a third person. Stick to a mutual examination of the facts and what they imply to both of you.

Stage 6: future targets

Agree on targets to be met during the year ahead. Be specific about them. Relate them to what has been accomplished during the previous year.

Stage 7: offering help

Review what you can do to be of greater help. Improvement is almost always a mutually dependent activity. It is likely that the teacher will approach the task with greater confidence and enthusiasm if you and he or she have jointly accepted responsibility for improvement.

You should be the best judge of how one of your teachers will take what you have to say. Try to anticipate people's reactions so that you are not taken by surprise. An appraisal interview is unlikely to be helpful if the head is shocked by a teacher's unexpected antagonistic or hostile attitude. By expecting specific reactions you can try to plan your responses well ahead. It may be that you will learn much about your own interpersonal skills in such situations. (In an honest interchange your own ego may well take a knock!) Careful forward planning in terms of the type of open-ended questions which you could ask will help you to feel confident and relaxed. The following questions will provide useful starting points for much discussion:

What aspects of your teaching have interested you most?
What aspects interest you least?
How do you feel you have carried out the main tasks you are responsible for?
What tasks do you feel you have performed particularly well and why?
What areas, if any, are unclear to you about any aspect of school life?
What extra help or guidance do you feel you need?
What can I do to assist in your professional development?
Where do you see your future in, say, three years time?

The appraisal interview can be seen as part of the school-based in-service training programme for teachers. Such a programme will have other necessary components, including:

1. A good staff library where occasionally certain books which are relevant to the school's curriculum or organizational developments are specially featured. Staff should be encouraged to read in order to inform others.
2. The facility for discussion on relevant issues. There are a number of types of discussion groupings, all of which may have a place, according to the school's general development policy. Some discussions may take the form of workshops, run by staff or visitors, whilst others could include a review of published materials, talks by colleagues, or general staff meetings.
3. A series of purposeful visits to other schools when specific ideas are being considered.
4. Opportunities for the production of written material by staff to act as guidelines for the development of all curriculum areas.

Delegating responsibility

Some heads are afraid to delegate responsibility even though members of their staff are paid an additional allowance to be specifically responsible for an area of the curriculum or school organization. There are heads who look upon delegation of authority and responsibility as a loss of control. It should not be like that and, in fact, the good head will delegate responsibility for work along with the necessary authority to carry it out, establishing the proper control measures which will allow for immediate corrective action to be taken if things go wrong. A checklist on control measures might be:

1. Is the teacher thoroughly trained, ready and willing to do the job?
2. Have you mutually agreed the nature of the job?
3. Have you delegated the responsibilities gradually or all at once?
4. Have you corrected mistakes and praised progress?
5. Can you intervene at any time without causing great upset?

The head can build the confidence of staff members by delegating the responsibility and the authority to carry it out. This gives them the concrete evidence that the head has faith in them and their abilities and will give the staff the chance to grow and to develop more confidence. Once responsibility has been delegated there is a need to develop the initiative of each member of staff, which can be accomplished by giving open-ended instructions to each teacher. Such an instruction tells a person what you want done, but it does not tell him or her how to do it. Open-ended instructions will give each teacher the opportunity to carry out the same task differently, according to his or her experiences and training.

An open-ended instruction is composed of three basic parts. First, state the problem to be solved clearly and concisely, and make sure it is understood completely. Second, the limitations imposed must be carefully outlined in order that members of staff know just how far they are free to try out their own methods. Third, spell out the resources available so that the teacher knows exactly what can be used to accomplish the job. In a good instruction of this type the head acts as the catalyst, leaving the main task for the staff to execute – this is the key to effective leadership.

If the head is going to hold one of the staff responsible for a particular task, then the head should also give the teacher the authority to carry out that responsibility. It is not possible to be responsible for arriving at a solution to a problem if you must go to someone else to get the authority to carry out your responsibility. In addition, the staff should realize not only what their responsibilities are, and what authority they have, but also that they are accountable to the head. Unless this last concept is understood, the head will not be able to achieve the desired results. All members of the staff must have a clear understanding of what is expected of them individually. They should know what their responsibilities are and just how much authority they have. Then, if mistakes are made, they can be corrected without hesitation. If a head is afraid to hold one of the staff accountable for results, then the consequences for their failure must be accepted by the head who, in turn, must be held responsible. A good head is one who knows when to take corrective action and when to offer praise for a job well done.

How you delegate responsibility is an expression of how you see yourself. If you have a good self-image you will not be threatened by the delegation of authority. Nevertheless, the delegation of authority requires very careful thought and planning – it is not an art that is necessarily easily acquired. To build a truly decentralized organization that succeeds in inspiring initiative, imagination, self-discipline and loyalty among the staff, the head must demonstrate four important personal attributes. He or she must:

1. Be receptive to other people's ideas.
2. Realize that people will make mistakes.
3. Be tolerant when let down by those to whom authority has been delegated.
4. Be able to exercise powers of self-restraint.

Once the head has mastered the art of delegation, there are four specific aspects to which attention must be paid if authority is to be effectively delegated at all levels within the organization of the school:

1. Jobs must be clearly defined and mutually agreed. Every staff member to whom authority is delegated deserves a clear written statement of their responsibilities. Within such job descriptions there needs to be a recognition that a scale-post-holder has to accept responsibility for a general quality of teaching and a leadership role throughout the school. There will be occasions when this will require involvement in other tasks outside those which have been specifically defined.
2. Goals must be set and clearly understood so that everyone knows which specific goals relate to every delegated task.
3. Ideas must be communicated to everyone at every level in the school to help them make the 'right' decisions.
4. Controls must be established. A good head can delegate authority to do a

task, but cannot be rid of the responsibility for getting the task done. Therefore, there must be ways of knowing what is done and of knowing when to step in and take action. You cannot have delegation without control.

Needs and motivation of staff

It hardly needs underlying that whatever his or her enthusiasm, expertise and competence, no head can be effective without well-motivated staff. It is the willingness of teachers and other staff to work hard, to throw themselves with enthusiasm into work, which makes organizational change possible.

From the work of Herzberg (1966), it seems clear that if you undertake to 'motivate' people so that the work will then be done better, you are on the wrong track. What is needed is the structuring of the work in such a way that the work will have the motivators in it. The work itself, then, will motivate people and the enterprise will have expanded its capability of achieving its objectives. That is the way to ensure the full utilization of teacher talents. The planning and organization of the work environment, therefore, is a key to successful school management, as it is to successful classroom teaching. An understanding of human motivation is important if you are to understand why people behave as they do, and it helps to understand your own behaviour.

There is a very extensive literature on the theory of motivation as part of the theory of learning. Maslow's pioneering work helps us to understand the pattern of human motivation. Motivation is not administered externally; it is the result of needs within us that cause us to act as we do. The general view starts with the belief that people tend to be most strongly motivated when certain needs are met. According to Maslow, we are first motivated by our physiological needs – for food, shelter and survival. Once these needs are satisfied, safety and security become the major motivators, then participation and roles in social groups and society, then status and ego satisfaction, and finally self-actualization. Clearly it is not assumed that everyone has each of the needs in equal strength. Some people may have one or more of the needs very strongly in evidence, while others have a quite different patterning of needs. Because people have different needs at different times they will respond differently to the same conditions. The theory is that while each person may have a unique profile of needs we each share the same set which go to make up that profile:

1. Affiliation: the need for a sense of belonging. Do all staff really feel that they belong in the school and are regarded as part of the team? The head's skills as a communicator are of great importance in meeting this need.
2. Achievement: the need for a sense of 'getting somewhere' in what is done. Do the staff feel that they are achieving things in the tasks they undertake? The head's ability to ensure that roles and responsibilities are clearly defined and understood will help people meet this need.
3. Appreciation: the need for a sense of being appreciated for the efforts one makes. This relates very closely to achievement – does the head show appreciation to the staff for both effort and achievement? People thrive on praise and it is probably one of the highest motivational factors – when did the head last offer praise to someone on the staff? Has the head praised all the teachers during the last term?
4. Influence: the need for a sense of having some influence over what happens within the work setting. The ability of the head to delegate effectively has considerable bearing on this issue. Staff do not wish or expect to have complete control over everything that happens in school but there are specific areas where they are able to lead their expertise and have some influence. Teachers are most highly motivated when they feel that they can contribute significantly to the shape of the curriculum.

In addition to these four basic areas of need, there is another closely related factor which influences teachers' motivation. This is self-concept. Each of us has a view of ourselves, of our abilities and potential, and of the sort of person we are, and of what we are capable of. This self-concept is developed over many years and is related very closely to the view of ourselves which we see 'reflected back' to us by others. None of us is very keen to attempt that which we believe to be impossible – to expend effort, time and other personal resources – unless we believe that we are reasonably capable of achieving worthwhile goals. Where you believe that you are not able to achieve goals set, or do specific things that may be required of you, then you are unlikely to try very hard – you will not be well motivated. The system may require you to try but it cannot force you to try hard. You tend not to be well motivated when asked to do that which is not consistent with your view of yourself and your capabilities – your self-concept. This is certainly an important factor to consider when attempting to change the curriculum responsibilities of a teacher on your staff. When groups of teachers have been asked to discuss strong and weak motivational factors within schools they have arrived at lists which strongly reflect the patterning of needs already discussed. The lists below, which have been compiled over recent years on in-service courses considering aspects of primary-school management, represent a sample of teachers' views.

First, teachers are *most* likely to be well motivated in regard to changes when:

1. They are involved in the formulation of the new approaches.
2. There is a feeling of 'solidarity'/community among the staff.
3. There is a demonstrable need for change.
4. Staff are confident of their own abilities to deal with an activity.
5. Skills for dealing with an activity have been fostered within teachers, or will clearly be developed in the future.
6. The head recognizes the extra time/effort put in by staff.
7. The head provides positive support and involvement.
8. The teacher feels generally secure within the school.
9. There is a sense that what is being done is also laying a foundation for future success.
10. As a venture, it is easy to join in at any time.
11. Clear educational and social goals are obvious.
12. There are regular discussions for the interchange of ideas, information and experience.
13. The previous experience of staff in comparable situations is utilized.
14. There is an open and friendly atmosphere generally within the school.
15. Teachers are sure of support in the case of difficulty being experienced.
16. The staff have confidence in the head, based upon his or her credibility and reputation for success.
17. The staff concerned have specific and clearly defined responsibilities.
18. A provision of time in 'working hours' is made.
19. The senior staff are actively involved in the work.

Teachers are *least* likely to be well motivated when:

1. They are simply told that they *must* . . .
2. They are put into a threatened position.
3. The activity is not well planned.
4. It is felt by teachers that the plan is a 'gimmick' promoted by a senior member of staff to further his or her own ends.
5. The teachers feel that the plan is mounted merely to satisfy higher authority.

6. A lot of hard work is involved without any apparent or obvious results.
7. Initial moves are badly organized, with consequent initial negative feedback.
8. The teachers feel alienated from the school or from whoever is responsible for the plan.
9. The head assumes the role of the 'expert', and there is a lack of opportunity for teachers to develop, or to exercise, responsibility.
10. There is group pressure from colleagues to 'opt out'.

The practical steps that a headteacher might take to increase the likelihood of the staff being well motivated include:

1. Facilitating early initial discussion within the staff.
2. Keeping overall control of the programme.
3. Developing staff, especially their skills, understanding and self-confidence.
4. Making available as much time as possible (and letting it be seen that he or she is doing so).
5. Leading by example.
6. Involving *all* staff, and not just teachers.
7. Providing aid, back-up and support, especially when there are particular difficulties.
8. Utilizing the skills and expertise of particular staff.
9. Making a very careful appraisal of the status quo, prior to committing the school to change.
10. Encouraging staff to suggest developments and modifications once the change process is under way.
11. Building up a system of steady, reliable support for teachers who are attempting to innovate in their own work.
12. Building upon success and not failure.
13. Delegating carefully; and delegating authority as well as responsibility.
14. Appreciating work already done, however trivial; not alienating those who are committed to the system which you may wish to change.
15. Not personalizing opposition – keeping it on a professional level.

Stripped of its essentials, good school management is appealing to the basic emotions of the staff. Teachers will want to do what the head wants them to do if they get what they want and need while they are doing it. The head holds the key to motivating staff, and only when staff respect and acknowledge the needs of their own position, and the needs of the school, will the head ensure loyal cooperation and full staff support. It is important that the head learns about the staff and their families, their hobbies and interests. As a head, demonstrate that you care for teachers as individuals: look them in the eye when talking to them and listen to what they have to say to you. Find at least one positive item to mention when you know that someone is discouraged or depressed. Always try to help your staff to achieve success in some small way so that they feel important and, above all, needed, whilst accepting that not everyone in your team is going to be a brilliant teacher.

There is little purpose in heads formulating a programme to develop the awareness and expertise of a staff of teachers until they have carefully considered their own interpersonal skills. According to Maslow (see page 97) (1968), in order to grow you must satisfy a variety of human needs. Interpersonal skills can be seen, from one point of view, as instruments enabling you to satisfy a number of your human needs. The skills of expressing yourself, responding to others, placing legitimate demands on others, and opening yourself up to being influenced by others, help you to satisfy safety needs (the need for a secure, orderly life) and esteem needs (the need for both self-respect and for respect from others). Successful interaction with other people requires the development of effective inter-personal skills. Therefore interpersonal skills are important not only to help you gratify legitimate personal needs but also to enable you to gratify the legitimate needs of others, work through interpersonal conflict, and estab-lish effective working relationships. You will need not only to know how to disclose yourself appropriately to others, but also to be aware of your characteristic ways of thinking and feeling about, and interacting with, other people. You will also need to recognize that your staff too will have different motivations, needs and aspirations. Not all will wish to involve themselves in development and its companion, change.

References

Herzberg, F. (1966) *Work and the Nature of Man*, Cleveland, Ohio: World Pub-lishing.

Maslow, A. (1968, 2nd ed.) *Towards a Psychology of Being*, New York: Van Nostrand-Reinhold.

Maslow, A. (1970 2nd ed.) *Motivation and Personality*, New York: Harper and Row.

CHAPTER 5

INNOVATION AND CHANGE: THE HUMAN FACTOR

At the heart of the headteacher's role is a responsibility for ensuring that every child and teacher in the school receives the best possible education. In order to achieve this, he or she needs not only to keep up to date with developments in both curriculum and in the understanding of effective teaching and learning, but to have the skill to enable his or her staff to do the same. Such information and new understandings will from time to time challenge the existing theory and practice of one or more members of staff, and it will be for the head to ensure that his or her particular leadership style provides the best possible spur and support for change. There are no known 'recipes' for successful change, but there are a number of different practices which seem to have achieved success in a variety of schools and other institutions; and these are all based on similar priciples of leadership, intervention and professional learning. It is the purpose of this chapter to discuss such principles in relation to innovation and change. The focus will be on what we have called the 'human factor' for two reasons: first, because change involves people in a re-examination of values, attitudes and feelings which, by definition, are not governed by rationality nor amenable to prescription; and second, because attempts to promote change are unlikely to meet with success unless there is an active consideration by the headteacher of the psychological and social dynamic in its planning, process, and evaluation.

> The wise old men were indignant. Their kindly smiles faded. 'If you had any education yourself,' they said severely, 'you would know that the essence of true education is timelessness.'
> (Benjamin 1939)

'Innovation' as used in this chapter refers to ideas or practices which are new or different from those which exist in the school and classroom; and the introduction and use of anything which is new implies change. So the focus for this chapter is change which is planned as a deliberate and collaborative process involving a change agent (head) and client (teacher), or group of clients, in solving a problem in order to increase the effectiveness of children's education. Change itself, whether major or minor, requires time, energy, skill and, most important, the commitment of the person who is being expected or encouraged to make the change. Problems of commitment arise especially where the need for change has been identified by someone other than the person expected to change.

The problem for the head or deputy head is how to achieve and support a commitment to change which will be more than 'token'. Rather than beginning, in this chapter, by describing various approaches or models which might be adopted, it is necessary first to investigate the likely psychological and social contexts which influence the attitudes of the teachers involved.

Professional learning

If we assume that professional development is a normal rather than an exceptional process, and that most teachers are capable of reflecting on their performances and improving them in the light of such reflection (Elliott 1976), then it follows that they are no strangers to innovation. Indeed, they are constantly having to take decisions about teaching which involve change. Some are immediate 'on the spot' decisions which are taken during the classroom action when there is no time for reflection; others are the result of a conscious thought process which occurs outside the classroom. These are 'reflective' decisions (Sutcliffe and Whitfield 1976).

It may be argued, however, that while these decisions are based on the teachers' identification of need, and while development of this kind occurs naturally and without intervention, such development is limited by the physical and social environment or context in which the teachers work and by their perceptions. For example, the classroom in which they work contains much more 'information' than they can handle, and their decisions about practice are concerned with finding ways in which they can survive, cope and teach effectively in a world which is stable. Thus practices are in a sense rules of action which allow them both to maintain a stable view of, for example, the classroom or the school, and to give priority to certain kinds of information while ignoring other kinds. They are theories of control. A new teacher very quickly develops assumptions about practices which allows him or her to cope with the complexities of teaching and being a member of staff. However, since it is rare for these to be made explicit or tested, the possibilities for evaluating these assumptions – which underpin his or her

1. Assess the situation (people, resources, constraints). For example, you may approach or be approached informally by individuals, or 'hear' a need voiced during a staff meeting, or initiate a staff meeting yourself.

2. Identify an area of concern (general or specific). The realization that there is a need for change may come through listening to staff and being aware of their thoughts, needs and relationships. If not, the ground has to be prepared for change. This will include planning how and when to implement change.

3. Communicate the concern informally to:
   (a) Headteacher/deputy headteacher.
   (b) Staff colleagues.
   (c) Other involved people e.g. parents/ancillaries.

4. Meet formally with colleagues to:
   (a) Identify the specifics of the problem(s).
   (b) Clarify issues.
   (c) Generate discussion of new ideas.
   (d) Decide on group aims and specific strategies: consensus-seeking; joint formulation of valid alternative strategies, leading to establishment of priorities and agreed deadlines.
   (e) Decide on ways of monitoring the implementation of the plan.

   } Negotiation of meanings

5. Implementation of the plan (with back-up provided, e.g. time, resources).

6. Revision of plan in the light of experience (a recognition that the logic of planning and the logic of action may not match).

7. Reflective appraisal of the effectiveness and new planning if appropriate.

   } Flexibility as a criterion of action

8. Consolidation of new pattern/plan.

9. Long-term evaluation.

Figure 5.1   Procedures in the management of change

teaching – are minimal. We have seen in Chapters 1 and 4 the need for reflection as part of a process of professional development.

To survive in a school it will be necessary for a teacher to accept into his or her system of behaviour the often unstated norms and expectations of the community and his or her colleagues in school. In the staffroom setting, for example, talk about teaching is governed by assumptions about the nature of talk about teaching. Thus, what happens in the classroom and what is said to happen in the classroom may be quite different, and it may not be surprising if the 'doctrine' of teacher as educationist is contradicted by the 'commitments' which arise in the classroom situation of teacher as practitioner (Keddie 1971).

So there are both perceptual and contextual constraints which may militate against teachers exercising their capacities to be self-critical and to identify problems. Indeed, all but the newest teachers are likely to have found their own personal solutions to problems shortly after entering the school. These enable them to strike a balance between opposing forces of teacher personality factors, ideological factors, presentation and nature of material, external requirements, and the characteristics of pupils (Lacey 1977). It is only when the teacher perceives that this personal solution is itself inadequate that he or she will be moved to search for means by which he or she can change.

It follows that a responsibility of the headteacher is to ensure regular opportunities for teachers to review their personal solutions.

Promoting change

Principles for the organization of opportunities for promoting change have been outlined, and indeed perhaps individual or collective staff discussions of these should be the first stage in the creation of a policy for innovation and change. One starting point is to embark on a programme of school or classroom evaluation which is preparation for and contributes to development. The case for school evaluation has been put by Simons (1981). The underlying assumptions for this are that:

1. better understanding of the organization and policies . . . could improve the opportunities and experiences provided in classrooms;
2. systematic study and review allows the school to determine, and to produce evidence of, the extent to which they are providing the quality of education they espouse;
3. a study of school policies can help teachers identify policy effects which require attention at school, department or classroom level;
4. many policy issues cut across classrooms and require collective review and resolution;
5. there are many learning experiences (fieldwork and extra-curricular activities, for instance), which do not take place in the classroom and which require the cooperation and appraisal of the whole school;
6. participation in a school self-study gives teachers the opportunity to develop their professional decision-making skills, enlarge their perspec-

1. The staff need to perceive the needs for change, and feel a responsibility for implementing and sharing in change, under good leadership (i.e. a need must be apparent to *all* those involved before change can begin).
2. The cooperation of the staff needs to be gained, and there must be good communication with staff who are directly and indirectly involved.
3. There is a need for the positive support of the headteacher.
4. There is a need for time to implement change.
5. There is a need for those involved to see benefits for themselves in addition to 'the school', for example.

Figure 5.2   Interpersonal relationships in change: motivation

tives, and become better informed about the roles, responsibilities and problems of their colleagues.

Normally, teachers (or headteachers!) cannot be expected to have the time or energy to engage in constant re-examination of their work. But there might be a policy in which, for example, teachers and groups of teachers agreed to focus their energy over a limited period on investigating a particular problem, applying a particular teaching method, or developing a specific aspect of the curriculum. Such an agreement is likely to produce commitment where a lack of one may only produce frustration.

There is a need for a policy because it is not assumed that change will be a continuous process, particularly where it involves self-evaluation:

> People have to develop implicit theories of action in order to make profession-al life tolerable. There are too many variables to take into account at once, so people develop routines and decision-habits to keep mental effort at a reasonable level. This evolution and internalisation of a theory of action is one aspect of learning to become a teacher and coping in the classroom. Hence to reverse the process and make the theory explicit for purposes of self-evaluation is to draw attention once more to myriads of additional variables, and to raise the possibility of paralysis from information overload and failing to cope . . . to continue for any length of time to treat all one's actions as problematic is a sure recipe for mental breakdown . . .
> (Eraut 1977a)

Whether the first priority identified by the staff of a school is to agree on a policy for staff development, whether it is to review curriculum, or roles and responsibilities, does not seem to us to be important. It is crucial, however, that the policy has been agreed through consultation so that all agree to commit themselves to the actions necessary to achieve it. The way in which this agreement occurs depends on the leadership style adopted by the head and the skills which he or she can apply.

Resistance to change

There is no assumption here that all innovation or change is for the better, nor that what is right for one teacher is necessarily right for another. As we saw in Chapters 1 and 4, teachers, like children, will be at different stages of development and have different needs; and these needs may be expressed through an apparent or real aversion to new ideas which involve them in change. Doyle and Ponder (1976) identify three types of response by teachers who are 'invited' to change:

1. The rational adopter – someone who might be said to adopt a step-by-step approach to solving problems. This person will:
   (a) Clarify goals and problems.
   (b) Collect information about how the problems arise.
   (c) Consider ways to resolve the problems.
   (d) Implement these.
   (e) Evaluate the success of the strategies implemented.
2. The Stone Age obstructionist – who neither accepts the need for change, nor responds to 'invitations' to be involved.
3. The pragmatic sceptic – who expresses 'a concern for immediate contingencies and consequences'. This person will evaluate change proposals in terms of their validity for him or her in his or her classroom. The pragmatic sceptic will ask three questions:
   (a) What do I/my pupils get out of it?
   (b) Can I relate it to what I do/how I teach?
   (c) What is its cost (in time, energy and finance)?
The pragmatic sceptic wants to see a return for his or her investment.

There may be connections between these responses and those of teachers influenced by their own career expectations and the broader political context of education. For example, many schools are faced with declining pupil populations, and diminishing financial resources. Staff find increasing difficulties in achieving promotion. There is more 'intervention' in school life by parents, LEAs and central government through calls for curriculum monitoring and institutional appraisal, and bids for more central control of the curriculum. The increase in internal and external pressures may lead to perceptions by teachers that there is less trust in their 'professionality'. The head may therefore have to help motivate some teachers who are frustrated, apathetic and resentful. Hand (1981) divided the teaching force of the 1980s into three categories:

1. Those who are frustrated in their ambitions.
2. Those who are happy to be in their final school posts.
3. Those likely to gain (further) promotion.

Not all schools will contain all of these clear-cut categories of teacher, and indeed these categories are not in reality mutually exclusive; people and contexts can and do change. However they do serve to draw the attention of headteachers and others concerned with innovation to the complex web of role expectations, institutional constraints, professional experiences, teaching attitudes and approaches, and personality factors, which may influence the responses of teachers to any form of new idea or practice that the head may wish to introduce into the school. After all, it is the head's responsibility, not the teacher's, to try to match individual and institutional needs; and there may often be conflict created by the tensions between the two.

It is important then, to move with care, particularly when new (innovative) practices are being suggested. (Even the introduction of regular staff meetings may require teachers to change other arrangements.) It cannot be assumed that rational discussion will convince 'Stone Age obstructionists' (Doyle and Ponder 1976) who neither accept the need for change, nor respond to the invitation to be involved. However there are a number of dimensions of morale in organizations which, when linked to assumptions that professionals wish to increase their effectiveness, may be used as guiding principles for motivation. Most teachers would wish to have (Miller and Fom 1966):

1. Intrinsic job satisfaction.
2. Involvement in the immediate work of the group which constitutes the school.
3. Identification with the organization.
4. Satisfying interpersonal relationships with 'superiors' and immediate colleagues in the organization.
5. Satisfaction from work status.

The starting point of innovation may focus on any one of these or other areas. Staff may wish to develop a language policy, to rethink the use of resources, to develop a system of staff responsibilities, update subject knowledge or investigate teaching methods.

1. Individuals like to have responsibility and be trusted.
2. To create a feeling of belonging in the school.
3. Support and encouragement to staff boosts morale.
4. It eases one's workload! (In the short term.)

NB Where responsibility is given, so must authority be.

Figure 5.3   Reasons for participation in change

The management task

Providing learning opportunities for staff as well as children

It is a prime management task to plan, support and monitor the innovation process, but not necessarily to initiate it. The head should provide environments which minimize constraints on learning, and in which a variety of concrete personal experiences may be reflected upon, talked about and assimilation or accommodated. Teachers need time for planning, and this may involve (temporary) changes in teaching or lesson organization which only heads are in a position to support – by, for example, taking a class (or classes) in order to release a teacher (or teachers) who wish to visit other classrooms or schools.

In organizational terms, this implies that the headteacher will ensure that regular opportunities exist for individuals and groups of individuals to:

1. Reflect on practice.
2. Share practice.
3. Identify issues for change which may arise from 1 and 2.
4. Generate alternative strategies for change.
5. Acquire the appropriate help to achieve this (human and material).
6. Apply the strategies.
7. Evaluate the processes and outcomes.

The emphasis so far has been on the teacher's felt needs. This is not to suggest that the head's needs are any less legitimate, but that like children, teachers may be best motivated when following their own interests and where the work is based on their own experiences. Eraut (1977) suggests that, 'The best way to promote teacher development may be to expect it, or at least to be careful that one's actions do not implicitly suggest that one does not expect it.' These principles have clear links with problem-solving client-centred models of innovation. These models place the client's needs at the centre of the learning process. The client is thus an active causal agent and participant at every stage of his or her learning. Our point then, is that where work is related to personal experience and perceived needs, and occurs in the context in which this experience and these needs occur (i.e. the classroom or school), the teacher will feel more involved and learn more.

It follows that the primary function of headteachers and 'leaders' in schools is not to identify need for others, *but to involve others in identifying needs*. This indicates a recognition that change which is based on the teachers' perceived need is of prime importance. The list of steps towards successful leadership given in Chapter 1 (page 18) is relevant here.

Asking questions

Whatever the starting point for change, the head will need to pose the following questions:

1. What help and support do individuals need from me? Can this be made available?
2. What help and support does the teacher/group of teachers need from
   (a)   inside
   (b)   outside the school?
   Can this be made available?
3. What are the priorities for action? (What is appropriate at this time, at this stage of development?)
4. Is the activity practical in terms of time, energy and resources?
5. What will the teachers gain from the activity? (Doyle and Ponder's (1976) 'pragmatic sceptics' will want to know what's in it for them and their pupils, and what the 'cost' will be.)

In effect, the asking of these questions is the beginning of the formulation of a policy for staff development within which innovation may occur.

Leadership roles

The general leadership stance taken by headteachers who achieve success in promoting change is consultative rather than directive or prescriptive. A distinction is being drawn here between authoritative and authoritarian. The former is built on agreement through negotiation; whereas the latter is built on the use of status alone. Although writing in a different context – that of evaluation – Macdonald's (1976) description of three 'ideal types' of evaluation study might equally apply to styles of leadership and intervention in schools:

1. Is the change short-term, with a quickly achieved goal?
2. Is the change long-term, involving continuity and spread through the school?
3. What is your estimated time scale? If a lengthy period then be aware of the need for continuity and progression through staff meetings, discussions, priorities and choices.
4. Do you lead by example?
5. Enthusiasm – are you aware of possible insecurity of staff?
6. Are you able to offer the support needed to all staff and especially to those who feel unsure?
7. Can you make sufficient resources available – are you aware whether additional resources will be needed next year, and whether this will mean a reduction in cash for other areas of the curriculum?
8. Will you offer the advantage of school time to allow staff to implement change (i.e. head teaches their class or takes a group)?
9. Do you use external help where appropriate? E.g.
(a)   Visits – in pairs to other schools; workshops.
(b)   INSET days as an integral part of a development programme.
(c)   Use of external consultants (from local university or college).

Figure 5.4   Thinking and planning questions

1. Bureaucratic – in which the key concepts are service, utility and efficiency, and in which the key justificatory concept is 'the reality of power'.
2. Autocratic – in which the key concepts are 'principle' and 'objectivity', and in which the key justificatory concept is 'the responsibility of office'.
3. Democratic – in which the key concepts are confidentiality, negotiation and accessibility, and in which the key justificatory concept is 'the right to know'.

There are clearly in-built difficulties of role definition for the headteacher who embarks on a 'democratic' style of leadership. Schools are not democracies, since the head, and not the teachers, has responsibility for the curriculum and standards of the school. The head writes references on the staff, so that there will inevitably be a power and authority gap. In cases where the head is non-teaching, there may also be a 'credibility' problem. Without denying the existence of these problems it is, nevertheless, possible for them to be minimized rather than emphasized by the way in which heads approach their leadership role. The role so far described is similar to that described by Havelock (1971) in a consideration of change agents' roles. It would involve the head in playing any one or a combination of the following three roles:

1. Catalyst – who prods and pressures the system to be less complacent and to start reviewing its work.
2. Solution-giver – who knows when and how to offer a solution appropriate to colleagues' needs.
3. Process helper – who can help colleagues in the 'how to' of change. (In a recent paper on in-service, Eraut (1982) asserts that much INSET, '. . . seems to assume that . . . knowledge use or process skills already exist; so the focus is on ideas which it is hoped the teacher will feel inspired to implement, without providing assistance with the process of implementation itself . . . ')

This last role is crucial if colleagues are to be given long-term support. Thus the process helper's task is to assist colleagues to:

1. Identify, define and clarify needs.
2. Generate alternative strategies and set objectives (which are 'realistic' in terms of time and energy commitments required and which have a 'pay-off' and relevance in the eyes of colleagues).
3. Acquire relevant resources.
4. Provide appropriate moral and intellectual support in the implementation of strategies.
5. Evaluate the success or otherwise of the process and solutions.

Affective relationships

Clearly, all those involved in promoting change must be concerned with the manner as well as the matter of change. Many programmes of professional development are based on what we believe to be a myth, that one can simply sit down with others, work out policies, aims, strategies etc, and implement them according to rational procedures based on apparently rational agreements. This does not take account of the fact that there may be conflicts over, for example, values, power and practicalities, an increase in workload, or a desire for old certainties.

In work which is concerned with questioning the teacher's self-image the affective relationship is of prime importance if one is to take into account such concerns as anxiety, status and identity. For example, as mentioned in

Chapter 1, changing one's teaching style may involve a temporary 'burden of incompetence' (Macdonald 1973) so that there will be a considerable need for psychological and moral support (Day 1981).

This affective area is rarely made explicit, yet the attitudes of teachers are clearly crucial to the success, not only of the process of innovation, but also of the interventionist. How is the headteacher perceived? Is he or she an authority or a threat? Is he or she a process helper or a judge with alien values? During the process of devising a policy and carrying it through, it is likely that the head, far from being non-directive, will play a variety of supportive roles. After all, he or she is as committed to the professional development enterprise as anyone, and so cannot hope to be a 'neutral' figure – except when playing a role of 'procedural neutrality' which '. . . expresses a teacher's commitment not to use his authority to promote judgments which go beyond impartial criteria of rationality' (Elliott 1975).

While it is important to build mutually supportive relationships with their teachers based on the commitment of both to enhancing the quality of education in the school, headteachers must be prepared to donate their experience and responsibilities in ways which are both appropriate to their role as head (with accountability to LEA and parents, as well as teachers) and to their role as a member of a team (with accountability to children and teachers). There will be times when some teachers may need to be 'told', or have an expectation that they should be 'told' or 'directed'; others when they should have some say in what and how they learn. Their perceptions may be formed by such factors as role expectation, socialization or psychological needs. Indeed, when adults are participants in their own learning, problems may arise because their inquiry skills are either underdeveloped or undeveloped. Among adults as among children, then, the need and ability to be self-directing will vary, and depend on factors such as cognitive and personality development, motivation, social development and role expectation (Day and Baskett 1982). It follows that *the head will need to be able to adopt a variety of roles*: he or she will at various times be acting as: an appraiser (of staff and pupil work); an adviser/counsellor (to staff and pupils); an organizer (of timetable, curriculum, resources); a linking agent (between staff within the school, between staff and other teachers, between staff and pupils, and staff and parents); an expert (on curriculum content or teaching techniques); a promotor (of an idea etc); a legitimator; or a devil's advocate (to test out commitment to a process or the logic of an idea). In effect the one individual is expected to be an innovator, a change agent, an evaluator and a friend!

The two main principles which seem to be fundamental to the intervention practices of the headteacher are:

1. The perceived needs of the teacher(s) are of paramount (though not sole) importance.
2. The interventionist's role is collaborative and co-equal, but not necessarily neutral or non-directive.

Interdependence rather than dependence or independence is thus a central feature in this process regardless of whether the change is focused on classroom teaching and organization, curriculum content, or school management and organizational structures.

A case study of change in a primary school

Most deputy heads and headteachers possess the capacity to act as change agents, but it is the extent to which they are able to acquire and apply the appropriate knowledge and skills that may determine whether their leadership is successful. Despite the need for skills in handling interpersonal relationships, and supporting teachers who have problems in changing, there are few opportunities available for heads and others to acquire them. The following is the description of a case study of innovation selected from the work of a group of sixty heads drawn from three counties who attended a recent management course.

The context

'After a few weeks as newly appointed head of this school, I felt that my first priority was to work with the two scale 2 post-holders the school had, so as to develop them as effective consultants and leaders for their curriculum areas. It had become clear that in the past, these people had been given no responsibility and were, therefore, not au fait with the role of the consultant.

'As an addendum to this, it seemed to me urgent that post-holders for language and mathematics be appointed: the language post had been unfilled for eighteen months and there had never been a maths consultant.

'The school had reorganized three years ago from separate infant and junior schools to a through primary. The junior head had been transferred to another reorganized primary school a mile away, and the infant head (who had already been in post for thirty years) had been made head of this school.

'A lot of unpleasantness had occurred before reorganization; staff having started grievance procedures against the junior head, who was trying without support in the school, to move the school along good modern lines. Fortunately for me, only two of these staff remained; one was to take early retirement at the end of my first term.

'The deputy head, who also came from the infant school, had been in post for more than twenty years, also having no effective role, other than class teaching.

'No curriculum meetings had been held for at least two years; there were no policy statements or guidelines to assist staff; no one had attended any INSET courses for over a year, and the work of the school, especially at the upper end, was textbook orientated and narrow. The site itself posed problems; there was no playing field, no proper hall and little space outside classrooms.

'On the positive side, however, the school had a good image in the community and standards of reading and computation were good. It therefore seemed vital to build on these, widening the curriculum as the staff gained confidence in me and my methods.'

The stages of working

'The main stages of the work were to work closely with the two post-holders, to involve the whole staff in curriculum discussions and guideline preparation, to give a lot of myself in teaching alongside colleagues and in practising what I preached by being first on the list for courses, and to involve the, at first, unwilling deputy in everything. Privately I had decided that if she could not or would not support me, she would be bypassed. The needs of the school could not be set at risk for one person. Finally, the staffing structure had to be finalized and posts filled.

'I spent much time in conversation with post-holders, discussing their roles and stressing the contribution they had to make to the effectiveness of the school. When they seemed easier with me and willing to voice their opinions, I asked them to jot down the following: what they did for their post, what they would like to do for it, and their priorities for it. They knew that I should be doing the same and that we would compare notes and agree a final draft later.

'At the same time I operated a form of blackmail by pointing out likely in-service meetings and courses to them, saying that I was going and would be glad of their company!

'Once the job specifications were agreed we looked at priorities and tried to fix a time scale to these. I stressed that I would support and help them but that I valued their contributions too much to do it all myself. Their reactions were interesting: one was very eager after a hesitant start and, unasked, prepared an outline plan for a curriculum meeting with the staff, to look at topic-based learning. This was light at the end of the tunnel! The other post-holder was very nervous and needed much support; he felt staff would take offence if he "tried to tell them what to do". When reassured on this he seemed to gain confidence, but then was absent for a week with "nerves". It was obvious that he was not yet able to fulfil the role I wanted. It was equally obvious that soon he must begin to fulfil his obligations or my whole plan for the post-holders could fail.

'At the same time the staff had been asked if they would give one evening a fortnight to curriculum discussion. This time was chosen because I felt it important to show that work doesn't end when the children go home. For the first term and a half I led these meetings and the first couple were hideously one-sided. They covered record-keeping (nonexistent before), planning of work, assessment and monitoring children's progress, and special needs. I continually stressed that I considered the staff to be professionals, that I welcomed their ideas and comments, and gradually a dialogue developed. It became clear, following visits to other schools and attendance at courses, that they felt the need to extend our work and they began to make suggestions and talk about their needs. The end of the tunnel got a little nearer!

'At this point, the post-holder for environmental studies and topic work held the discussion he had planned earlier. He began with a 'brainstorming' session on what we hoped to achieve in topic work, leading on to our needs in resources and guidelines. I sat back during this discussion to stress what I had been saying about responsibility of post-holders.

'From this meeting and the following ones, our guidelines on project work and its planning and resourcing were drawn up, and a scheme for recording children's work was completed.

'At this stage, our "nervous" creative arts consultant was tackled again. To his credit he said he was amazed at the staff's response and felt he'd like to begin. I felt that his series of meetings needed much moral support from me and that he needed to plan very carefully, knowing what he wanted from the discussion. He decided he'd like to know what staff needed in the way of resources, whether they would welcome guidance in the use of new materials and techniques and some ideas towards art and craft guidelines. To his credit, after a shaky start, the meeting developed well, staff contributing usefully and agreeing that they welcomed his help. New materials were ordered and a series of technique workshops took place. Guidelines are now being completed.

'In the meantime it had been agreed that a post for a language consultant would be advertised locally.

'Staff seemed more used to my spending much of my time in their classrooms, mainly on language work, and it seemed that they were using me as language consultant. The time had come when the inevitable request was made for me to take groups of slow readers. This I refused. I stressed again that teachers were professionals and therefore had responsibilities to *all* the children in a class. What I did do was to hold a series of workshops on strategies for helping reading difficulties and to make certain that the necessary materials were available. I also asked the local educational psychologist for assistance and his response was most helpful. Finally, I took classes to free teachers to work with slower learners.

'I felt it was now time to look at the gaps still in the curriculum; it had disturbed me for some time that little or no science-based work took place. Therefore, at a curriculum meeting I asked for staff's ideas on what the primary curriculum should cover. The response was pleasing and included science. Objections were that there was no equipment and many of them felt unable to teach it. Further discussions and a course based on the 'Look' and 'First Look' scheme followed. We felt the scheme would be a 'crutch' and therefore agreed that we would begin with it as a 'core' but would branch out from it later. The environmental studies post-holder very quickly resourced it and everyone made a conscious effort to include science in their classroom work.'

Reflections on the process of change

'During this first year of headship I have increasingly felt that it is very easy to work in isolation. Therefore, it cannot be assumed that staff know the thoughts and wants of the head. A constant dialogue must take place and the school's hierarchy has a role here.

'I conscientiously tried to involve the deputy head in all planning whether she wanted to know or not. I have made situations where she had to become my mouthpiece although this slowed things down. In fairness, this is no longer the case. I have done the same with consultants so that the plans I have for this school are known and shared.

'I have also seen that staff find the arrival of a new head disturbing; they feel as if they are "under the microscope". Therefore if change is to take place, it must be planned and relatively gradual. My staff had to spend time getting to know me and my ways; therefore a period of "marking time" had to exist while they gained confidence in me and I got the feel of the school and assessed priorities.

'While the process of change was going on, I had to realize the potential stress it occasioned. Staff had to be supported, encouraged and frequently thanked and praised. I had to develop eyes that saw everything new, however small, so they could see I was noticing their efforts.

'Since change in a school involves people, we had to have some leeway to modify our plans and we had to be able to say if something was failing and change direction. This was my hardest lesson: I had to develop enough confidence to be able to change direction. On reflection, I should be glad that I had this to do since it meant that other people's ideas were being added to mine. For example, having instigated the changes already described and feeling that we were working to capacity on these, I was approached by the deputy who said she wanted to 'enrich' the maths teaching for infant children. In the absence of a maths consultant, she was prepared to lead this herself. I felt it was crucial to use this new initiative, but was concerned that this would overburden my colleagues. My last worry on this was that the deputy was not capable of the task she wanted to set herself. After consultation with all the staff involved we decided to go ahead.

'This project is still under way and it would be wrong at present to call it a success. It is, however, of major significance in that it showed that our deputy had started to view the school as a whole and had recognized one of its weaknesses. Further, she had decided that she was prepared to lead the work. This alone was a great step forward and it showed me that she and I could work together, which I had doubted.

'Now, with changes occurring in three curriculum areas and consultant staff fulfilling the roles I wanted for them, it was time for me to look again at the support I could give them. It seemed to me that since everyone was now used to having me in the classroom, working with them, they would not find it inhibiting to have other colleagues as well. Therefore we planned to set aside one day per consultant per half-term when I would free them from their classrooms to work with others. I said that I would want to know in advance how they would use the time and would need to be told of its outcome. This has been in effect for a term and a half and is working well.

'Finally, six weeks ago, an existing member of staff was promoted to maths consultant, giving the school the staffing structure I had intended.

New blood from outside in the person of the language consultant helped things along enormously. This teacher did not need to get used to my ideas on the role of the consultant; we shared the same ideas and she accepts the responsibility eagerly.

'There is still a long way to go. The changes that are still to occur will probably go more smoothly. My approach will be improved in several ways: I no longer "pussyfoot" when I see something I dislike because I feel that our staff know I value them as professionals. If, therefore, they fall short of this standard, I feel they can expect to know about it in no uncertain terms. My confidence in myself has grown; it matters less to me now if I make a mistake and have to change direction. It is probably good for staff to know that this can happen. I no longer feel that I have to plan and lead everything, so I can now make use of the informal working party such as the infant maths group. In effect, for the future, I shall lead less from the front and more "from the middle".

'I am also confident enough to make far more use of outside assistance. In the beginning I hesitated before asking an Inspector to assist in change; now I feel able to ask them to put their ideas in the melting pot. I no longer expect to have all the ideas and answers myself. What I must not lose sight of is the overall development I want for the school. Our staff is not a democracy and never will be; it therefore is still of vital importance to discuss plans thoroughly with all involved and retain the "casting vote". It will therefore become even more important to strike the right balance between doing it alone and involving staff to the full. As always, I feel that an open and constant dialogue holds the answer. Time will tell!'

The case study presented in this chapter describes processes of innovation and change. These processes occurred in the context of an emerging policy of overall curriculum development, and the next chapter seeks to provide further insights and practical approaches to the management of the curriculum.

References

Benjamin, H. (1939) Foreword *in* Peddiwell, J.A. *The Sabre-Tooth Curriculum, in* Hooper R. (ed.) (1971) *The Curriculum: Context, Design and Development*, Edinburgh: Oliver and Boyd in association with The Open University Press.

Day, C.W. (1981) *Classroom-Based In-Service Teacher Education: The Development and Evaluation of a Client-Centred Model*, University of Sussex Education Area, Occasional Paper no. 9.

Day, C.W. and Baskett, H.K. (1982) Discrepancies between Intentions and Practice: Re-examining Some Basic Assumptions about Adult and Continuing Professional Education, *International Journal of Lifelong Education* vol. 1, no. 2.

Doyle, W. and Ponder, C.A. (1976) The Practicality Ethic in Teacher Decision-Making, *Interchange* vol. 8, 1977.

Elliott, J. (1975) The Values of the Neutral Teacher *in* Bridges, D. and Scrimshaw, P. (eds.) *Values and Authority in Schools*, London: Hodder and Stoughton Educational, 1975.

Elliott, J. (1976) Preparing Teachers for Classroom Accountability, *Education for Teaching*, journal of the National Association of Teachers in Further and Higher Education, no. 100.

Eraut, M.E. (1977) Strategies for Promoting Teacher Development, *British Journal of In-Service Education* vol. 4, nos. 1 and 2.

Eraut, M.E. (1977a) Accountability at School Level: Some Options and their Implications *in* Becher, T. and Maclure, S. (eds.) *The Politics of Curriculum Change*, London: Hutchinson, 1978.

Eraut, M.E. (1982) What is learned in In-Service education and how, *British Journal of In-Service Education*, vol. 9 no.1.

Hand, G. (1981) First Catch your Adviser: The INSET role of advisers, *in* Donoughue, C. et al. (eds.) *In-Service: The Teacher and the School*, London: Kogan Page.

Havelock, R.G. (1971) The Utilization of Educational Research and Development, *British Journal of Educational Technology* vol. 2, no. 2.

Keddie, N. (1971) Classroom Knowledge, *in* Young, M.F.D. (ed.) *Knowledge and Control*, London: Collier-Macmillan.

Lacey, C. (1977) *The Socialisation of Teachers*, London: Methuen.

Macdonald, B. (1973) Innovation and Competence, *in* Hamingson, D. (ed.) *Towards Judgement: the Publications of the Evaluation Unit of the Humanities Curriculum Project 1970 — 2*, Centre for Applied Research in Education, Occasional Publication no. 1, pp. 88 – 92.

Miller, D.C. and Fom, W.H. (1966) *Industrial Sociology*, New York: Harper and Row.

Simons, H. (1981) Process Evaluation in Schools, *in* Lacey, C. and Lawton, D. (eds.) *Issues in Evaluation and Accountability*, London: Methuen.

Sutcliffe, J. and Whitfield, R. (1976) Decision Making in the Classroom; An Initial Report, *Research Intelligence*, vol. 2, no. 1, BERA.

CHAPTER 6

MANAGING THE CURRICULUM

This chapter is not about the curriculum itself, but about the practical approaches schools can make to managing the teaching and learning processes. Like the other chapters in the book, this proceeds from the assumption that the process of managing is a collaborative activity in which all members of the teaching team work together as co-managers, each with their particular role to play and responsibilities to exercise, but united under a common purpose. Essentially, the chapter is about the ways in which the crucial interaction of teacher and pupils within a learning environment can be affected by the process of management. The emphasis is thus practical and a variety of participatory exercises which may be adapted to suit the reader's particular situation and purposes are included.

Learning experiences result both from the formal programmes of work initiated by teachers and from a wide variety of informal factors often referred to as the hidden or covert curriculum. In this chapter curriculum is used to refer to all planned activity involving teachers and pupils and to teaching methods and approaches.

It is not enough simply to think of a curriculum as a set of policy documents and guidelines. A wider concept of the curriculum was firmly established in the Schools Council Working Paper 70 *The Practical Curriculum* (Schools Council 1981):

> . . . there is a need for a visible structure for the curriculum. A useful starting point is to consider each pupil's right of access to different areas of human knowledge and experience. The heart of the matter is what each child takes away from the school. For each of them, what he or she takes away is the effective curriculum.

This paper thus emphasizes a view of the curriculum as the experience each child has at school and what each takes away.

Much of the activity that has been undertaken in schools under the name of curriculum development over recent years has been about the formulation of desirable objectives. The classroom lives of learners have been little affected, as the study of Barker Lunn (1984) has demonstrated. In fact this research into junior classrooms suggested that teaching methods and practices have changed far less significantly than has often been thought.

A working model

Managing the curriculum can be considered as a process consisting of three key stages:

1. Planning: working out the educational philosophy of the school.
2. Operating: defining, implementing and controlling the learning processes.
3. Evaluating: determining how well the philosophy has worked in practice.

Each of these three broad processes will be discussed in detail, but before this it is important to stress again that the chapter is about how the curriculum is managed, not about what that curriculum should be. The emphasis will be placed on the way the staff as a whole can work together to provide a cohesive approach to classroom work, the ways in which they bring their collective hopes, expectations and experiences to bear in formulating and implementing decisions about the direction in which the school needs to go, and how they create a working climate conducive to professional growth and development.

Such working conditions are not easy to create and maintain. They are most likely where there is a happy balance between task and process. This requires the recognition of the three key factors described in Chapter 2 – the task itself, the needs of each individual and the needs of the team as a whole (Adair 1983). Much will depend upon the headteacher's capacity to maintain a purposeful concentration on the tasks in hand while at the same time providing sensitive and encouraging support to individuals. Keeping the team as a whole informed and motivated is also necessary, especially if particular tasks only involve certain members of staff.

Planning

This stage of the curriculum-managing process is essentially one of making policy. This does not imply simply the manufacturing of complicated documentation about discrete practices and procedures but rather the creating of agreements about the purposes of the school and the means of bringing them to reality. It is unlikely that effective learning will be achieved unless all staff have a clear sense of direction and share a common vision of what they wish to achieve.

In Figure 6.1 it is suggested that the process of curriculum management is a cyclic one in which the outcomes of previous plans and policies are used to inform the need for new ones. In most schools planning is an activity which is often very much a question of adaptation and development. Only those teachers fortunate enough to be given the somewhat rare privilege of setting up an entirely new school have the opportunity to plan without the limiting constraints of existing tradition and practice.

Before embarking on any policy-making activity it is important to be aware of the factors which influence and determine the way that schools tend to go about the business of organizing learning. Four particular factors have been suggested as especially significant (Whitaker 1983):

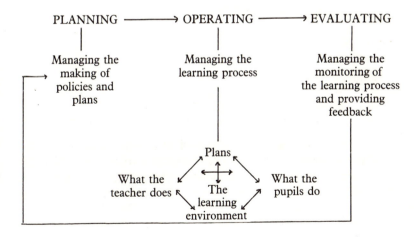

Figure 6.1   Managing the curriculum – a working model

1. Prescriptions – what we must do.
2. Expectations – what we should do.
3. Situations – what we have to take account of here.
4. Predilections – what we would like to do.

Few curriculum prescriptions exist, although current trends point to the possibility of further legislation as the debate about the 'entitlement' curriculum proceeds. There is some evidence that where there is prescription, in religious education for example, many schools ignore it (DES 1985). Yet despite this lack of central direction of the curriculum it is interesting that schools are characterized more by their similarities than their differences. Most primay schools subscribe to the same half-dozen or so subjects and the learning process is characterized by a preoccupation with basic cognitive skills (Barker Lunn 1984, DES 1985).

If prescriptions are few, expectations exist in abundance. The way most schools go about their business is more determined by what they think they should do than what they know they must. In other words, a wide range of influencing factors combine to channel schools in a particular direction. Some of the key determinants can be summarized as expectations deriving from:

1. Traditional educational practice.
2. Assumptions about how children learn.
3. Received wisdom about what schools should be like.
4. Public experiences of the education system.
5. Informed opinion.
6. Public debate.
7. Teacher training.
8. Assumptions about what classrooms should be like.
9. Assumptions about how teachers teach.

Progressive trends in education are viewed with some suspicion and the affairs of the William Tyndale school in Islington in 1976 (Auld 1976) and the subsequent public enquiry set in motion a 'back to the basics' movement which, despite receiving no official support or encouragement, continues to affect the policy-making of schools (Barker Lunn 1984, DES 1985).

The third set of factors influencing planning and development are those related to the particular circumstances of each school. These will include building design, previous curriculum history, the pattern of organization, the attitudes of parents and the community, and the composition and attitudes of the teaching staff.

Many heads approach their first headship with grand plans in mind. Their predilections often stretch beyond mere curriculum development to a total transformation of the whole educational enterprise. Angela Anning (1983) has suggested that the management strategies of headteachers take a well-defined course. First comes an environmental impact. The head makes all sorts of improvements to the surroundings – plants appear in the entrance hall and drapes accompany displays of objects. The second stage involves the writing of curriculum guidelines. Mathematics and language are usually tackled first, those for dance, drama or art and craft rarely being accomplished. After this, Anning suggests, heads arrive at what she describes as Beechers Brook. This is the realization that despite all this effort, what goes on in the classroom between the teacher and the children has hardly changed at all. To affect this requires management activity designed to change fundamentally the way that staff approach and conduct their professional business. In most cases Beechers Brook is too awesome even to attempt to jump.

This is not to disparage what heads find themselves doing, but it does emphasize the difficulties that face the agent of change in education. Individual predilections may have meaning for particular class teachers, but headteachers' predilections inevitably involve change in other people rather than themselves. In preparing for innovation in school there are four key factors which are likely to influence success (Whitaker 1984):

1. An awareness of how individuals behave.
2. An awareness of the sources of power within the school, and how they operate.
3. An awareness of the values system of the school.
4. An awareness of how the proposed change will affect each of these factors.

(For a more detailed discussion of these factors see Chapter 5.) This list suggests that in successful managing, awareness is everything. In terms of the planning stage of curriculum management there are some clear implications which relate back to the point about leadership being concerned with the task, the individual and the team. If policy-making is to be successful it needs to respond to individual needs as well as to those emanating from the staff as a whole. It is the staff itself, working together, which has to become the power source of policy and decision-making. The policies and decisions that are made need to reflect a value system that has been forged by the working team through a process of questioning assumptions, challenging beliefs and synthesizing experience.

There may sometimes be a tendency to tackle curriculum development without first paying attention to the four factors listed above. A sense of direction is difficult to achieve when there is not only disagreement about the route but arguments about whether the journey is necessary in the first place. The skill in management lies in harnessing the creative forces of those who in the end have to deliver the new policy. Therefore before planning the details of the learning process it is necessary to tackle the question of philosophy and values.

School philosophy and values

The following exercises are recommended as possible ways of approaching this issue. They are best undertaken as whole-staff activities after some work has been done to build a trusting and participative co-managing climate in the school.

Exercise 1

The first task attempts to deal with the four sets of determinants referred to above – prescriptions, expectations, situations and predilections. The printed sheet illustrated in Figure 6.2 should be given to all members of staff meeting together. It is important to undertake this activity as a collective experience since it is one of the ways in which cooperative and participatory skills can be developed.

Staff should be invited to complete the form individually, allowing about 10 – 15 minutes. When this has been done ask them to work in pairs to share each other's responses. Allow a good 20 minutes for this. It is likely that some fundamental issues will be raised by this questionnaire, issues that perhaps do not often get an airing in staff meetings. The next stage, numbers allowing, is to join pairs up into foursomes. Each group's task is to produce a further sheet listing responses on which there is broad agreement – factors which each of the four can subscribe to. A small group of staff members can than be invited to take responsibility for producing a draft statement summarizing the factors affecting school philosophy and practice. Copies of this draft can be circulated for further discussion before being formally adopted.

The way in which this exercise is conducted is very important. As a task it is designed to facilitate whole-staff interaction and cooperation. What goes

Under the four headings below list the factors which you consider affect school policies and practices
1. Prescriptions – what we must do
2. Expectations – what we should do
3. Situations – what we have to take account of here
4. Predilections – what I should like to do

Figure 6.2   Factors affecting school policies and plans

on in the pairs and foursomes can help create a good climate for open and creative decision-making. For the head, who is likely to have responsibility for facilitating the activity, the question of pace and timing is crucial. It is vital not to inhibit free and open discussion by hurrying the stages of the exercise. On the other hand, providing some time constraints does help to generate a keen sense of purpose. A useful technique is to suggest a time limit of, say, 20 minutes for the paired discussion, and then to offer a 5 minute extension if the talk seems active and productive.

The exercise described above could well occupy a number of hour-long staff meetings. When much of the work is being conducted in pairs and small groups it is useful to allow 15 minutes or so at the end for an open session when all staff can share their thoughts and feelings about what has been going on. This should not be too rigorously 'chaired'. Reticence will

1. Children learn best when . . .
2. The pupils I like best are those who . . .
3. It is important that children . . .
4. When I think about the children I teach . . .
5. The children I most worry about are . . .
6. I don't like children who . . .
7. What I want my pupils to acquire is . . .
8. What children really need is . . .
9. The qualities I most admire in pupils are . . .
10. What we should really be emphasizing in the curriculum is . . .

Figure 6.3   Questionnaire: values and beliefs about learners

soon be overcome if contributions are accepted and valued. This exercise will have aired the issue of the purposes of education.

Exercise 2

Curriculum planning will also need to be informed by a clear understanding of how the staff view the learning process. In particular it is essential to tease out what the various beliefs are about how children learn. This next exercise is designed to do this, by helping teachers get in touch with how they feel about the learning process and the pupils they teach. The questionnaire, illustrated in Figure 6.3, should be duplicated and a copy given to each member of staff. Working on their own the teachers should be invited to complete the sentences, not thinking too hard about them but responding fairly quickly and intuitively.

After allowing a reasonable time for completing the sentence stems, staff should then work in pairs. The talk should focus first on the process of answering the questions: which ones were difficult, or maybe seemingly impossible, and whether any of them actually caused discomfort. The talk should then move on to sharing responses to the questions themselves. The same procedure as in the previous exercise can then be adopted, with staff working in pairs and then as a whole group, attempting to bring together the various value positions. Again a small group can be asked to prepare a summary draft for discussion.

Exercise 3

The third exercise is one to clarify philosophy and values. It attempts to synthesize the outcomes of the previous two activities. Following consideration and discussion of the draft summaries comes the task of forging these outcomes into a coherent form. This exercise is best carried out in a room where large sheets of paper can be stuck or pinned to the wall. Three large sheets of paper should be prepared for the meeting, headed, respectively: What we hope for our pupils; What we believe in about learning; What we believe in about teaching.

Working as a whole group, or smaller ones if the staff is larger than eight, the idea is to 'brainstorm' responses to each of the headings. It is important to sustain the rules of brainstorming – all responses are valid and are recorded and there is no discussion about items offered. When the lists are complete the staff should divide into three, each small group taking one of the lists. The next stage is to classify and categorize the responses, providing headings for each classification. The summary documents from the previous exercises should also be produced and items from these added to the lists. The classified lists should then be photocopied and distributed for further discussion and refinement.

These various summary documents should provide enough material to form the basis of a very thorough and comprehensive statement of the educational philosophy of the staff. This does not have to be a lengthy well-argued document but can be more a set of statements setting out the values and beliefs which underwrite school practices and procedures. It is a good idea to aim to produce a statement short enough to form the introduction for the school booklet for parents.

The learning process

Having considered some ways to reach agreement about basic school philosophy and values, the next stage is to consider how the daily work of the school can be planned. To facilitate this it is useful to adopt a conceptual model that closely reflects the ideas and values that have previously been agreed. Many such models exist and schools are faced with rather too many to choose from. Certainly one of the new pressures on schools in recent years has been the regular and sometimes concentrated publication of documents about the curriculum. These now form a central part of those determining factors summarized above under the heading of 'expectations'. For the head and staff of a school, one of the problems is what to believe. Although the plethora of curriculum documentation contains many common themes it also represents variety and divergence of approach. If a school does decide to adopt a model presented in one curriculum document it cannot be sure that a few months later another document will not come along with a different emphasis and an alternative set of priorities. The school has to decide which of the following courses to take:

1. Choose a particular document and follow its suggestions.
2. Stick to a school-based approach and make adjustments where necessary in response to published evidence.
3. Look at available documentation and develop a flexible and pragmatic working model that has the capacity to respond to new challenges and changed situations.

Whichever approach is adopted it is important to underwrite it with some clear assumptions about the nature of curriculum change and development. Three particular assumptions seem necessary:

1. Curriculum development should not be regarded as a once-and-for-all event but as a natural process of dynamic growth.
2. In the changed and changing times that we now work in, flexibility of management systems and structures is crucial. If the system is rigid and unbending the strains will be felt by all.
3. Change needs to be seen as the natural order of things. We should expect that it will become increasingly necessary to do things differently as circumstances change and as we learn more about the learning process in our school and about what works well for learners and what does not.

For the staff of the school involved in curriculum management, the implications are clear. It is vital to adopt a working model which reflects the school as it is now and takes account of current values. It is also necessary to resist the temptation to plan for a distant vision – a school in an ideal world. Above all, it is essential to see the management of the curriculum as a constant cycle of planning – operating – evaluating, a process closely linked to the roles and responsibilities that teachers occupy and also to a clear policy for staff development.

The wide variety of approaches to curriculum management can be illustrated by reference to four key documents published in recent years (Figure 6.4). A comparison of these particular approaches to curriculum design demonstrates just how varied is conceptual thought on the subject.

Document	Approach	Example
Primary survey (DES 1978)	Subject based	Aesthetic and physical education: 1. Art and crafts 2. Music 3. Physical education Language and literacy: 1. Reading 2. Writing Mathematics Science Social abilities: 1. Social, moral and religious education 2. Geography and history
Aims into Practice (Schools Council 1975)	Personal growth	Development: Intellectual Physical Aesthetic Spiritual/religious Emotional/personal Social/moral
Primary Practice (Schools Council 1983)	Subjects and approaches	Science Mathematics Language and literacy Past and present Imagination, feeling, sensory perception Personal and social Topic work Assessment and records Organization Staff development Evaluation
The Curriculum 5–16 (DES 1985)	Issues and concerns	Breadth Balance Relevance Differentiation Progression

Figure 6.4 Approaches to curriculum management

One of the outcomes of the subject-based approach adopted by the HMI survey of 1978 (DES 1978) was a tendency to return to a more formal differentiation of subject matter and to initiate the 'back to the basics' trend mentioned earlier. This was despite the strictures contained in the report that pupils achieve more successfully in basic subjects when they have access to a broad and rich curriculum.

The *Aims into Practice* project (Ashton et al, 1975) boldly conceived of the curriculum in terms of growth and experience, suggesting that learning programmes could more successfully be determined through reference to the six areas of human development. It was unfortunate that this particular project was underfunded and that more effort was not made by the Schools Council to carry out a comprehensive dissemination programme.

Primary Practice (Schools Council 1983), following the lead of *The Practical Curriculum* (Schools Council 1981), related a broadly subject approach to the key issues of assessment, organization, staff development and evaluation. This recognizes the essential practical nature of curriculum management and warns of the dangers inherent in the tendency to separate curriculum and methods.

Most recently the HMI publication *The Curriculum 5 — 16* (DES 1985) has attempted to conceive of the curriculum in both conceptual and practical terms. By placing emphasis on the need to apply checks for breadth, balance, relevance, differentiation and progression, this is another document to recognize the essentially pragmatic quality of curriculum management.

For those involved in the daily process of school management, confusion and frustration are created by the lack of consistency in these official reports and documents. Schools cannot be blamed for failing to take notice of the urgings of officialdom if the messages they are receiving lack clarity and consistency. In practice, of course, such publications do provide food for thought and sometimes help in the development of practical strategies. The wise school is one that adopts an essentially eclectic approach, taking from these sources that which relates well to particular circumstances and needs. A management process which is flexible has the capacity to respond to new ideas without having to compromise previous activity or abandon hard-worked-for agreements.

One of the most important functions of planning for learning is to create a clear and cohesive action plan for bringing school philosophy to life in the classrooms. What is missing from many curriculum policy documents and guidelines is a modus operandi – a way of organizing learning experiences to

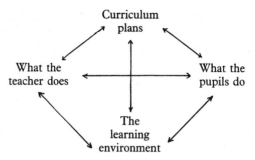

Figure 6.5 The learning process

realize purposes and intentions. This takes the issue of curriculum planning into the classroom and into matters of teaching style and classroom organization.

Figure 6.5 suggests a framework which conceives of the learning process as a dynamic interaction of four key factors. By separating out these key ingredients it becomes possible to provide a simple yet comprehensive approach to planning. For each class teacher the task becomes one of making decisions about the relationship between learning intentions, teacher behaviour, pupil behaviour and the environment in which that relationship is developed. Such decisions have traditionally been left to individual class teachers, and the making of agreements about teaching methods and approaches has not traditionally been regarded as a significant part of curriculum planning and management. What is now being suggested is that such agreements are a central part of that key process and that effective learning cannot be planned for if the essential practical factors in that process are not part of school policy-making.

Knowledge about teaching and learning

Teachers must be encouraged to identify questions to ask of themselves and to devise procedures which will enable them to collect and record relevant information. The desire for particular changes in curricula, organization, teaching strategies or assessment procedures may emerge from this. Realistically, however, it cannot be expected that all teachers will be able to undertake the sort of comprehensive scheme of self-evaluation through programmes of action research outlined in Chapter 7. Indeed, it has been argued that such commitment to self-disclosure should occur only from time to time. Assuming that in practice only a relatively small part of teacher time can be made available for systematic practical reflection and analysis, it is most important that intellectual and moral support is provided throughout, and that opportunities to engage in appropriate in-service activities are provided.

The notion of 'leading professional' is often used to describe the head of a school, and one area in which this concept can be usefully applied is in assisting teachers to consider the implications in general terms for pupil learning of the use of different planning and teaching strategies. Clearly particular uses will depend on particular purposes, and no one way is necessarily any better or worse than any other. However:

> Values are involved in education not so much as goals or end products but as principles implicit in different manners of proceeding and producing . . . in my view, many disputes about the aims of education are disputes about principles of procedure rather than 'aims' in the sense of objectives to be arrived at by taking appropriate means . . .
> (Peters 1968)

It is worth while, therefore, highlighting briefly how some of these values are communicated through planning, pupil tasks and their negotiation, and teacher – pupil interaction.

Many teachers claim that they plan for 'discovery-learning' experiences for pupils, yet it is worth considering that within this term two distinct models may be identified, each with different planned processes and outcomes:

1. Learning by discovery (or 'guided discovery'), in which the teacher has pre-specified content objectives, e.g. certain knowledge and principles to be learned. Here the teacher will tend to use non-instructional means to achieve his or her ends, e.g. guessing or 'information' games.
2. Learning to discover (or 'inquiry based') where the emphasis is on the process of how to inquire rather than on the product of past inquiries. Here students are involved in learning procedures for critically evaluating knowledge and principles, leaving what is to be learned as an open matter (Schulman and Keisler 1966, Elliott 1973).

The amount of teacher dominance over classroom events may be related to the characteristics of pupil-task activities rather than the personal characteristics of teachers. Depending on the degree of control exercised by the teacher over the subject matter, the pacing, and the direction of the task, pupils will be discouraged or encouraged from:

1. Valuing their ability to make decisions, creating and shaping knowledge, and becoming their own experts in thematic content.
2. Forming and testing hypotheses about themselves and others and the signs and symbols used to create, express and communicate meaning.
3. Viewing the teacher as a keeper and controller of knowledge.
4. Viewing themselves as uninformed acolytes, passive knowledge-receivers who are dependent on the teacher for their learning.

In the classroom itself teachers might observe how much time they spend talking in relation to pupil talk. Are their conversations one-way? What is the language which they use? If it is mainly functional, what opportunities for learning about language are being denied to pupils? Does teacher 'busyness' in the classroom (Sharp and Green 1975) mean that they are spending more time with those articulate pupils who demand attention than others who appear to be quietly 'getting on with it'. One of the questions which is asked by Bassey and Hatch (1979) concerns the differences between long and short interactions:

> Is it the case in your classroom that short interactions mainly serve to keep everyone busy, while long interactions are more valuable as teaching events? Would it be more desirable to have more long interactions?

Such issues as those above and others raised by Barnes (1976) and others, should be core reading for all engaged in managing the curriculum.

A useful way into the debate about teaching style and classroom management is to use some of the very interesting analysis from the ORACLE project (Galton and Simon 1980). This examination of primary classrooms identified three basic teaching styles – instructing, enquiring and monitoring – which involve teachers working either with the class as a whole, or with small groups or individual pupils. A high proportion of teachers use a combination of all three approaches but often with an emphasis on one in particular. Before agreements can be made to adopt common approaches in the classroom it is necessary to conduct some wide-ranging discussions about how teachers are already carrying out their teaching. Much will depend on the confidence of individual teachers but the following strategies are possible approaches.

Describing experience

A series of staff meetings can be held in each teacher's classroom in turn and the teacher can be invited to describe:

1. How the classroom is organized.
2. How learning experiences are managed.
3. The range of learning experiences of the pupils.
4. The range and variety of teacher behaviour (perhaps using the ORACLE categories).
5. Styles of presentation.
6. Expectations about standards.
7. Basic approaches in particular curriculum areas.

Observing practice

Although staffing constraints can make it difficult it is very helpful to create the possibility of teachers spending some time in colleagues' classrooms observing – not observing to evaluate but observing to inform. Following general discussions among the staff as a whole a programme of observation can be drawn up so that all teachers have the opportunity both to observe and to be observed. The purpose is very much to help the teacher who is observed although it is likely that the observer will gain considerable insights into the learning process by observing it closely and in some detail. One of the best ways to conduct such a programme is to ask teachers to draw up a list of factors in their classroom work they would like more information about and to use the observer to gather evidence. The following examples serve to illustrate the range of possibilities of this strategy:

1. Observing an individual pupil and recording behaviour.
2. Observing a group of pupils undertaking a task.
3. Monitoring pupil interactions.
4. Observing in a particular area, e.g. the book corner or science bay.
5. Monitoring the teachers' interactions with specified pupils.
6. Monitoring the teachers' use of instructional language.
7. Monitoring use of resources by pupils.

An observation of an hour can provide considerable data for a most useful professional conversation as the observer provides feedback on what was observed and the observed teacher seeks clarification about it.

Generating checklists

Working together in meetings, staff can build a variety of checklists to assist classroom analysis. These can be in the form either of questionnaires or of the sentence stems used in Figure 6.3. The lists could refer to a whole range of factors. Perhaps a good start could be made by inviting the staff to brainstorm factors under the following headings:

1. The classroom.
2. What the teacher does.
3. What the pupils do.

Staff could undertake to complete one checklist per day for a week. The next meeting could then be used to share information and to see how wide a divergence of practice there is between teachers. This will provide much material for discussion and planning. A technique similar to this one is referred to in Chapter 7.

A practical approach to curriculum management

The activities and procedures that follow are designed to help the head and staff keep the curriculum under review. They constitute a practical approach which conceives of curriculum management in terms of five key factors. Attention to these ensures that the whole process of managing the learning is systematic. Each of these factors is dealt with separately in the form of a series of practical activities. Together the five sets of activities constitute a package which can be applied in whole or in part to the educational life of a school. The activities are offered as examples, and each is capable of considerable expansion and modification to suit particular circumstances, and as new ideas are developed and new needs identified. It is the general approach, rather than the specific contents, that is important. The activities can usefully be presented in a working folder, a copy of which is held by each member of staff. The five factors for consideration are:

1. The teacher.
2. The pupils.
3. Aims and objectives.
4. Teaching style.
5. Classroom organization.

1. The teacher

Activity 1: 'Myself as a teacher'   This questionnaire (Figure 6.6) has been designed to help teachers get in touch with how they feel about their work in the classroom and to raise issues about the values they incorporate in their work. The exercise is best handled when the staff are meeting together as a

1. What I most like about myself as a teacher is . . .
2. I am at my best in the classroom when . . .
3. My pupils like it when . . .
4. I would describe my teaching style as . . .
5. When I think about my classroom I . . .
6. I like it best in teaching when . . .
7. I should like to change the way I teach but . . .
8. The main change I should like to make in my classroom is . . .
9. What I have most to learn about teaching is . . .
10. What I most try and avoid in my teaching is . . .
11. I envy those teachers who . . .
12. I am the sort of teacher who . . .
13. When somebody criticizes my teaching I . . .
14. What I would really like to see happening in my classroom is . . .
15. What I most dislike about being a teacher is . . .
16. Children seem to learn best when I . . .
17. I wish I was better able to . . .
18. Most of my colleagues think I am . . .

Figure 6.6 Questionnaire: 'Myself as a teacher'

group. Each member of staff should be invited to complete the sentences and then to talk them through with a colleague. In fact the approach is very similar to the one described earlier (page 128).

It is useful if staff keep their questionnaires and their responses and make a note in their diaries to return to them in about six months. The questionnaires could then be completed again and responses compared with earlier ones. There will be much fruitful discussion arising from the changes that can be detected and from any new themes that have begun to emerge.

Activity 2: 'Myself as a learner'   This is a similar exercise but is designed to focus on the nature of learning in the teachers' own lives. The procedure is the same as that in Activity 1. (Figure 6.7)

Activity 3: Effective teaching   This exercise provides an opportunity to

1. I have found learning most enjoyable when . . .
2. The teachers I have learnt best from have been . . .
3. When I succeed in my learning I feel . . .
4. Things I would like to have learnt but failed to do so . . .
5. One specific learning goal I have is . . .
6. I can learn on my own if . . .
7. My particular skills as a learner are . . .
8. I sometimes avoid learning because . . .
9. The most recent thing I have learnt is . . .
10. What I should most like to learn about myself is . . .

Figure 6.7   Questionnaire: 'Myself as a learner'

consider the various factors which contribute to effective teaching. The activity should be conducted as follows.

1. Provide each teacher with fifteen small index cards.
2. Ask the teachers to use five cards to write down the five areas of professional knowledge that are most important in teaching.
3. The next five cards should be used to list the most important skills in teaching.
4. The final five cards are for the most important qualities in teachers.
5. Spread out all the knowledge cards and invite staff to categorize them, putting similar cards in a pile. A new card can be written to incorporate a composite statement, which represents these.
6. These cards should then be pinned to a large sheet of paper in an arrangement agreed on by the staff. This pattern should reflect the relationship between the different categories of 'knowledge' statement accumulated.
7. Do the same for the 'skills' and 'qualities' cards.
8. The creation of these posters should provide considerable potential for staff discussion and negotiation. Certainly it will generate consideration of a wide range of issues associated with the learning process.
9. The outcomes of the discussions, both formal and informal, will have many implications for staff development, the allocation of roles and responsibilities, the process of change within the school and curriculum planning.

2. *The pupils*

Activity 1: Traditional assumptions   This activity is designed to help teachers consider the learning process from the pupils' point of view. This can be done by examining the sorts of assumptions that underlie the learning process in schools. Carl Rogers (1983) has suggested that the following assumptions about learners have become firmly rooted in the schooling system:

1. Pupils cannot be trusted to learn.
2. An ability to pass examinations is the best criterion for selection and judging potential.
3. Evaluation is education; education is evaluation.
4. What a teacher teaches is what a pupil learns.
5. Knowledge is the accumulation of content and information.
6. The truths of subjects are known and must be learnt.
7. The way a pupil has to work is more important than what is being studied.
8. Creative people develop from passive learners.
9. The 'weeding out' of the majority of pupils is the best way of producing the well educated.
10. Pupils are best regarded as manipulative objects, not as people.

Working in small groups (or as a whole staff if there are fewer than six), the teachers should be invited to take each assumption in turn and consider what evidence there is in the school of the presence of that assumption. Evidence that is accumulated will provide much food for thought, discussion and decision-making.

Activity 2: Good learners   It is important for teachers to have clear ideas about the qualities that are to be encouraged in learners and for these to be shared and feature in the school's curriculum policies. The brainstorming of the characteristics of good learners can be followed by comparing it to this list compiled by Postman and Weingartner (1971). Good learners:

1. Enjoy solving problems.
2. Know what is relevant for their survival.
3. Rely on their own judgment.
4. Are not afraid of being wrong and changing their minds.
5. Are not fast at answering; they find out and think first.

6. Are flexible in their learning.
7. Have a high degree of respect for facts.
8. Are skilled in enquiry.
9. Do not need to have a final irrevocable solution to every problem.
10. Are not depressed by saying 'I don't know'.

Activity 3: Pupil feedback It is important for teachers to be sensitive to pupils' reactions to learning activities and experiences, and to take account of these in managing the curriculum. A useful staff exercise is to design the sort of sentence-stem questionnaires illustrated above for pupils to complete. These can focus on a wide range of school issues from arrangements for break times to the detailed responses to particular classroom experiences. Other sorts of pupil evaluation sheets can also be designed and tested in order to find effective ways to incorporate pupil views into the scheme of things.

3. Aims and objectives

Activity 1: 'Primary Practice' Unlike many of the documents issued in the wave of curriculum publishing in recent years the Schools Council Working Paper 75, *Primary Practice* (Schools Council 1983), offers a whole range of strategies for curriculum management. In particular there are many procedures for planning the nature and the shape of learning activities. Case-study material is offered to provide much useful discussion material and there are checklists and questions on specific issues. The document has much to recommend it as a practical resource for curriculum management.

Activity 2: Flow charts Most teachers in primary schools are familiar with flow charts as aids to planning in topic work. They also have considerable potential in planning the more detailed aspects of classroom management, particularly when there are time factors involved and the sequencing of events is important. Flow charts are essentially the working diagrams of the creative process and therefore have a valuable part to play in a wide range of management activities. They can be used in the initial stages of planning to develop ideas, and in the final stages to work out ways to conduct the implementation of new procedures.

Any issue of current concern to the staff can be used to conduct a trial run with flow charts. They make an imaginative alternative to written discussion papers, offering scope for originality of design and use.

My problem is . . .	
I hope to overcome it by . . .	
My particular aim is . . .	
My first objective is . . .	What:
	How:
	When:
Statement of intent: I shall . . .	

Figure 6.8   Planning change

Activity 3: Planning change   When changes to the established order of things are being planned, it is very important that careful thought and consideration is given to each aspect of the innovation. The planning sheet illustrated in Figure 6.8 can be used on those occasions when it is necessary to be very clear about the steps to be taken in introducing an element of change, either in professional behaviour or in the management of the classroom.

4. Teaching style

Activity 1: Oracle   One of the most illuminating studies of the primary classroom has been that carried out by Maurice Galton and his colleagues at Leicester University (Galton et al 1980). Using close observational techniques the research has revealed a wealth of information about what goes on in primary classrooms. A study of the teaching styles revealed by the research and of the pupil types present in all classrooms should be high on the agenda for discussion in all primary schools. A whole range of management exercises can be built from the information produced by the project and a study of this research is highly recommended.

Activity 2: Process factors   Curriculum management needs to give a high priority to various factors which affect the learning process. The key ones of these have been summarized in *The Curriculum 5 — 16* (DES 1985) as:

1. Breadth – the extent to which pupils have access to the full range of learning experiences and opportunities.
2. Balance – the extent to which each area of learning is given appropriate attention in relation to the others and the curriculum as a whole.
3. Relevance – the extent to which the learning experiences provided by the school meet the present and prospective needs of the pupils.
4. Differentiation – the extent to which the learning experiences cater for individual needs and differences.
5. Progression – the extent to which the learning experiences relate to each other as part of a continuous process.

An important management activity for the head and the staff is to design ways in which these factors can be built into the three key managing processes – planning, operating and evaluating. As it stands, the list provides a useful check to apply both to the curriculum as a whole and to the detailed and practical plans teachers make to bring the curriculum to life in the classroom.

Activity 3: Teacher behaviour   An important element of teaching style is the sort of interpersonal behaviour adopted by teachers in the classroom. Research has suggested that it is the way in which teachers relate to pupils that is particularly important in promoting effective learning in pupils. Three particular behavioural qualities have been found to be especially significant:

1. The teacher's ability to understand the meaning classroom experience is having for each pupil.
2. The respect the teacher has for each pupil as a unique and separate person.
3. The ability of the teacher to engage in a genuine person-to-person relationship with each pupil. (Rogers 1983).

Pastoral care of this kind is a key consideration in any school. Its importance in primary schools relates especially to the role of the class teacher and the ways in which pupils are helped to overcome any difficulties in their personal lives as well as in their learning. A key part of any staff-development programme should be a consideration of how the qualities listed above can be developed. Agreements about desirable strategies for teaching should give high priority to these key characteristics. The following questionnaire shown in Figure 6.9 will help teachers to focus on this issue.

5. Classroom organization

Activity 1: The learning environment   It is a useful exercise for teachers to consider why they arrange and organize their classrooms as they do. One way to focus on this issue is to ask each member of staff to draw a scale plan of their classroom and to show on it the disposition of furniture, the location and storage of resources and equipment and the presence of display. Used in

---

1. Upon which assumptions about my pupils do I base my teaching?
2. What are my criteria for effective learning?
3. What proportion of my teaching involves active learning by my pupils?
4. How well do I sense the meaning that classroom experience is having for my pupils?
5. How do I show my pupils that I respect them?
6. How much of myself do I disclose to my pupils?
7. How well do I listen to what my pupils have to say to me?
8. What sort of praise do I give, what sort of encouragement?
9. In what ways do I judge my pupils?
10. How well do I understand the self-concept and its importance in the learning process?

Figure 6.9   Questionnaire: person-centred teaching

conjunction with the activity on pages 135–6 this activity can provide an opportunity to consider the following questions:

1. Which particular criteria about learning have determined the layout of furniture?
2. Does the arrangement of furniture suit all learning activities?
3. How does the arrangement of furniture affect pupil interaction and movement?
4. How were the decisions made about where resources would be located and stored?
5. How are resources distributed, collected, checked and made available to pupils?
6. To what extent has the classroom been organized to create special areas, such as a book corner, facilities for imaginative play, or an area for science and technology?
7. For what purposes are displays in the classroom arranged?
8. What are the criteria for displaying the work of pupils?

The more that staff can discuss the answers to these sorts of questions with each other the greater the opportunity for developing agreements about priorities and practices in the school.

Activity 2: Visiting other schools   Most teachers enjoy visiting other schools and seeing how colleagues approach their work in a different setting. Visiting schools is an important part of good staff development but consideration needs to be given to procedure. Whenever possible staff should visit in pairs. The opportunity to discuss the visit and its particular implications is very important and should not be underestimated. A key management activity for the staff when a programme of visits is being planned is to draw up a checklist of factors upon which information is sought. These are often best phrased as questions to which the visit will supply answers.

Activity 3: Encouragement to learn   This activity focuses on the extent to which classroom organization is designed as a learning environment which can itself encourage learning. Staff can be invited to look at their classrooms and list responses to the following questions:

1. In what particular ways does the classroom and what is arranged in it provide opportunities for the curiosity of the pupils to be stimulated and satisfied?

2. In what ways does the classroom as an environment motivate children to learn?
3. How does the organization of the classroom facilitate the pupils' access to essential resources and equipment?
4. How does the classroom facilitate and encourage interactions between the pupils?
5. What back-up facilities are provided so that there is a range of alternative activities for pupils to choose from when set work is completed?
6. How does the classroom reflect the learning of the pupils?
7. How are the pupils involved in the management of the classroom?
8. How are the pupils involved in creating new ideas for developing the classroom as a learning environment?

Managing the curriculum of the primary school is essentially a practical activity. Far too often it is seen as a theoretical exercise divorced from the learning lives of the pupils and the practical activities of their teachers. This chapter has attempted to provide both a theoretical perspective on curriculum management and a practical guide to carrying it out. The activities and exercises are only examples of approaches and are offered as ways into the process of collective and participatory management which underpins each chapter in this book. As exercises they are designed to create and stimulate staff interaction and discussion. If nothing else they will produce a great deal of lively professional debate which is a prerequisite of effective and dynamic curriculum management.

References

Adair, J. (1983) *Effective Leadership*, London: Pan Books.

Anning, A. (1983) The Three Year Itch, *Times Educational Supplement* 24 June 1983.

Ashton, P. et al (1975) *Aims into Practice in the Primary School*, London: Hodder and Stoughton.

Auld, R. (1976) *William Tyndale Junior and Infant Schools Public Enquiry*, London: ILEA.

Barker Lunn, J. (1984) Junior School Teachers: their methods and practices, *Educational Research*, vol. 26 no.3.

Barnes, D. (1976) *From Communication to Curriculum*, Harmondsworth: Penguin.

Bassey, M. and Hatch, N. (1979) A seven-category interaction and analysis for infant teachers to use themselves, *Education Research* vol. 21, no.2.

DES (1985) *The Curriculum from 5 — 16 — Curriculum Matters 2 An HMI Series*, London: HMSO.

DES (1984) *Education Observed — A review of published reports by HM Inspectors*, London: HMSO.

DES (1978) *Primary Education in England*, London, HMSO.

Peters, R.S. (1968) Must an educator have an aim? *in* Peters, R.S. (ed.) *Concepts of Teaching*, London and Windsor: Macmillan and Nelson.

Galton, M. et al (1980) *Inside the Primary Classroom*, London: Routledge and Kegan Paul.

Galton, M. and Simon, B. (1980) *Progress and Performance in the Primary Classroom*, London: Routledge and Kegan Paul.

Postman, N. and Weingartner, C. (1971) *Teaching as a Subversive Activity*, London: Penguin Books.

Rogers, C. (1983) *Freedom to Learn for the 80's*, Columbus, Ohio: Charles E Merrill Publishing Company.

Schulman, L.S. and Keisler, E.R. (eds.) (1966) *Learning by Discovery: a critical appraisal*, Chicago: Rand McNally & Co.

Schools Council (1981) *The Practical Curriculum — Schools Council Working Paper 70*, London: Methuen Educational.

Schools Council (1983) *Primary Practice — Schools Council Working Paper 75*, London: Methuen Educational.

Sharp, R. and Green, A. (1975) *Education and Social Control*, London: Routledge and Kegan Paul.

Whitaker, P. (1983) *The Primary Head*, London: Heinemann Educational Books.

Whitaker, P. (1984) *The Process of Change*, Leicester: Personal Learning Associates.

CHAPTER 7

EVALUATING TEACHERS AND SCHOOLS: A PROFESSIONAL DEVELOPMENT CONTEXT

While much work in schools goes on under the general headings of 'curriculum' and 'professional' development, 'evaluation' (unless related to the assessment of pupils) has often been ignored or at best implicit in this work. This chapter places evaluation within the context of professional development, recognizing that it is a crucial element in an individual's and a school's accountability procedures. It attempts to provide the reader with a detailed consideration of the issues involved in what the authors see as a complex task. It provides up-to-date information on means of establishing procedures and policies for school-centred evaluation; and suggests ways in which individual teachers may be assisted in systematically evaluating their own thinking and practice.

. . . the most important justification for undertaking school self-evaluation is to enhance the professional image and practice of teachers and schools. The current accountability climate may provide a context and impetus for the development of forms of evaluation but . . . schools may be tempted to respond to externally imposed schemes by producing what is required without themselves using the data for review of the professional practice of the school. If schools initiate evaluation in response to their own needs (and these may include producing accounts for outside audiences) these efforts are likely to be more sustained, to reflect the actual experience of schools and to lead to a quality control which is in the hands of those who have the prime responsibility for educating children and running the schools . . .
(Simons 1981)

There can be no doubt that evaluation is already a part of the practice of most teachers and schools. However, much of this occurs on an informal level and is characterized by its 'dependence on casual observation, implicit goals, intuitive norms and subjective judgment' (Stake 1967). Because of this, while it may sometimes be penetrating and insightful, it may also at times be superficial and distorted. The purpose of this chapter is to assist headteachers and others involved in leadership roles in their thinking about the principles and practices of school and classroom-based evaluation. Although this kind of evaluation will have as its prime purpose the improvement in the quality of teaching and learning in school, teachers and schools find themselves increasingly in a position where they must take account of an educational, economic, social and political world which has come to be dominated by the term 'accountability'. The chapter also attempts, therefore, to set evaluation in the context of three kinds of accountability and to assert that accountability and professional development need not be incompatible (Nuttall 1981). While 'genuine accountability is established by the obligation to self-monitor performance' (Elliott 1978), the chapter suggests that self-monitoring which is 'audited' either by colleagues in the school or from outside is more likely to result in accounts of practice which both contribute to the professional development of schools and teachers and are acceptable to interested parties in and outside the school than that which is not.

The HMI survey of Primary Education (DES 1978) asserted that it was important, '. . . to make full use, on behalf of schools as a whole, of teachers' strengths to build on the existing knowledge of individual teachers . . . However the requirements of society come to be formulated, teachers have the main responsibility for responding to them.' Certainly the opportunity for individuals and institutions to engage in evaluation must underpin any curriculum or professional development work which may be undertaken at school or classroom level. How, otherwise, may we proceed or make decisions about future work if we cannot judge where we are now, and how worthwhile our past endeavours have been? So the need for evaluation would appear to be self-evident. Indeed, it may be argued that most teachers and schools are already involved daily in evaluation processes through events such as staff meetings, curriculum workshops, pupil records, job descriptions, appraisal interviews (see Chapter 4), in-service events and even informal conversations with colleagues. Nor should we forget the 'on-the-spot' evaluations carried out by teachers in their own classrooms. These evaluations may cause teachers to change the direction and even content of their teaching according to their perceptions of their own effectiveness or the response of their pupils.

This chapter, while acknowledging the value of all those activities described above, seeks to raise issues concerning evaluations of teachers and schools which involve the systematic 'collection and provision of evidence on the basis of which decisions can be taken about the feasibility, effectiveness and educational value of curricula' (Cooper 1976). The types of decision for which evaluation data may be collected are (Cronbach 1963):

1. Course improvement – deciding what teaching material and methods are satisfactory and where change is needed.
2. Decisions about individuals – identifying the needs of the pupil/teacher for the purpose of planning his or her instruction, judging pupil/teacher merit for the purpose of selection and grouping, acquainting the pupil/ teacher with his or her own progress and deficiencies.
3. Administrative regulation – judging how good the school system is, how good individual teachers are.

While these points define purposes for evaluation, the means used for achieving these purposes are crucial to the effectiveness of evaluation in terms of teacher learning and real changes in practice resulting from this learning.

The views expressed in this chapter are based on the assumption that learning is most likely to occur if the following conditions are met:

1. There are opportunities for reflection.
2. There is internal commitment to the process of learning (not just the products).
3. There is freedom of choice for the learner.
4. Learning occurs in response to questions which are identified and confronted by the learner.
5. Learning occurs in response to the collection of valid information.

All these imply a need for teachers and schools to be involved at all stages of evaluation design, procedures and reportings, and this raises issues of contracting, negotiation, confidentiality, control and ownership of information collected. Before moving to discuss these it is necessary to take into account the psychological and social climate in which evaluation may occur; for no plans for evaluation, however well laid, will come to fruition unless staff are motivated and see the value of the activity for themselves. Teachers and schools must be ready and willing to engage in evaluation, and it must be recognized that this will not always be the case. Indeed, schools and teachers are likely to be in different 'states of readiness'. Attitudes of teachers may range from enthusiastic through to antagonistic. Thus, a prerequisite for successful engagement in the process of individual and collective evaluation is the nurturing of a climate which is conducive to it.

Contexts of evaluation

There is little doubt that the use of the term 'evaluation' often evokes negative responses by teachers. The reason for this is that it is perceived as something which is:

1. Usually initiated and carried out by someone else in an authority position.
2. Usually something done to someone (passive), often without agreement as to the standards, criteria and processes being used.
3. Usually for the purposes of making judgments in which weaknesses are highlighted.
4. Usually not providing support for long-term remedial work where required or requested.

So evaluation – even if we can understand the reason for it – is not always seen to be helpful. At the very least it means that we must disclose something more of ourselves to others than we would like or are used to. After all, teachers are trained to be 'professionals'. Once they qualify they are regarded as competent, and, by implication, able to plan, teach and evaluate their work. They are immediately given responsibility for a class of children and, apart from any who undergo planned induction processes, are 'left to get on with it', with the occasional visit by outsiders and, in more enlightened schools, headteacher, colleagues and parents. So although teachers are engaged daily in evaluating their pupils, by tradition it is rare for the teachers themselves to be evaluated by anyone other than themselves.

It is likely, then, that teachers will operate on a model of restricted professionality. Once they have developed a personal solution to any problems of teaching which they perceive – and this is usually achieved without any systematic assistance from others – it is unlikely that this solution will again be significantly questioned. Argyris and Schon (1976) characterize this pattern of teacher development as 'single loop' learning, in which theory-making and theory-testing is private. In a world of restricted professionality, professionals protect themselves and colleagues by speaking in abstractions without reference to directly observed events. This has the effect of both controlling others and preventing others from influencing oneself by withholding access to valid information about oneself. These effects are manifested in the 'Stone Age obstructionists' (Doyle and Ponder 1976) and other forms of resistance to change described in Chapter 5.

Formal evaluation which involves others clearly threatens this world of restricted professionality. The American educator Ernest House summed up neatly the ambivalent attitude which most of us hold:

> The first observation I want to make is that there is no real demand among teachers and administrators for evaluating their own programs. To evaluate kids, yes, we cannot live without that; but to evaluate ourselves and our own programs – no. At times, in that strange ideology with which we disguise our motives and cover our tracks, we educators convince ourselves that we would be overjoyed to receive data about our teaching and educational programs. Well, try it sometime. Try evaluating a program. On simply asking teachers their goals, we have had them break into tears and throw chalk across the room. Rare events, but not unrepresentative of teachers' attitudes towards evaluation.
>
> After all, what does a teacher have to gain from having his work examined? As he sees it, absolutely nothing. He is exposing himself to administrators and parents. He risks damage to his ego by finding out he is not doing his job as well as he thinks he is. Perhaps worst of all he risks discovering that his students do not really care for him, something a teacher would rather not know. The culture of the school offers no rewards for examining one's behaviour – only penalties. Since there are no punishments for not exposing one's behaviour and many dangers in so doing, the prudent teacher gives lip service to the idea and drags both feet. And this is not so strange, is it? Do we have any serious evaluations of lawyers, or doctors, or cabdrivers? That there is no such demand is a corollary of a broader principle: No one wants to be evaluated by anybody at any time. Evaluate an evaluator's work and see how he reacts.
>
> (House 1972)

So where evaluation of teachers is not *by* teachers it is not surprising that it is often seen as an unhelping activity to schools and teachers. This perception has been exacerbated by the 'hostile' environment in which many teachers perceive themselves as living. With increasing government intervention in the curriculum (see Chapter 6), more parental involvement (see Chapter 8), diminishing resources, fewer opportunities for promotion, a plethora of HMI and DES documents calling for curriculum review, and calls from employers for new conditions of service linked to salary structure, it is understandable then that some teachers feel threatened.

Accountability

The East Sussex Accountability Project (1979) identified three kinds of accountability:

1. *Answerability* to one's clients, i.e. pupils and parents (moral accountability).
2. *Responsibility* to oneself and one's colleagues (professional responsibility).
3. *Accountability* in the strict sense to one's employers or political masters (contractual accountability).

Although the three overlap, we may say that in recent years the emphasis has moved from 'responsibility' to 'answerability' and 'accountability'. However, these need not always be mutually exclusive, and the exemplification of the facets of accountability provided in the East Sussex Accountability Project supplies a clue as to how professional development, evaluation and accountability may be linked in practice (Figure 7.1).

The prime means by which a school may demonstrate its accountability to parents and the LEA, whether in terms of 'preserving and enhancing general levels of performance' ('maintenance' procedures in Figure 7.1) or through, 'the detection and amelioration of individual points of weakness' ('problem-solving' mechanisms in Figure 7.1) are the domestic monitoring of standards and regular review of staffing, curricula and teaching arrangements (Box 3, Figure 7.1). While there is no doubt that these do occur, they must be seen to occur and be communicated. As has been observed:

> In the case of schools, the teaching profession might demonstrate that they had procedures, of which self-evaluation could be a major component, to keep the quality of education under review, and with enough teeth to ensure that changes were made when needed.
> (Nuttall 1981)

So far it has been argued that leaders in schools have a professional, moral and contractual responsibility to ensure not only that evaluation occurs but that it is seen to occur, and that the results of evaluations are communicated in appropriate ways to appropriate audiences. (The issue here concerns both the form(s) of the communication(s) and the kind of information communicated.) As part of this, a climate of trust, support and openness must be established in which innovation may be encouraged and in which the learning needs of teachers as well as children must be considered (see Chapters 1 and 4). The assumption is that the central purpose of evaluation

	Answerability (to parents)	Responsibility (to self and peers)	Strict Accountability (to LEA direct or via managers)
Maintenance	1: – Regular communication on individual children's progress (via written reports etc.); – Accounts of overall policy (via prospectus etc.). Explanation of curricular aims and methods; – Reports on general standards of performance, academic and other (via open days, speech days etc.); – Encouragement of better parental awareness of school's activities and endeavours (via ready access to classrooms and staff, atmosphere of open enquiries and discussion).	3: – Domestic monitoring of standards; – Regular review of staffing, curricula and teaching arrangements; – Promotion of good relationships with parents (via school social occasions etc.); – Promotion of good relationships with feeder and receiving (secondary) schools; – Promotion of good relationships with managers, advisers, and LEA as a whole.	5: – Observation of mandatory and constitutional procedures; – Meeting of centrally agreed specifications; – Openness to authorized visitation; – Readiness to justify curricular goals and methods and overall policies; – Readiness to account for pupil performance standards.
Problem-solving	2: – Notification to all parents of complaints procedures; – Prompt acknowledgement and investigation of parental complaints, confirmation of action taken; – Early disclosure to parents, where appropriate, of problems (i) relating to individual children (ii) involving wider issues.	4: – Screening of individual children at risk (via internal reporting, pupil records, tests, etc.); – Provision of remedial help to children in need; – Awareness of incipient points of weakness; – Anticipation of potential crises.	6: – Reporting of unresolved external complaints and grievances; – Reporting of unresolved internal difficulties; – Development of effective means to deal with problems arising.

NB: The entries above are not intended to be comprehensive. They are meant only to indicate possible expectations or demands in each category. They should *not* be taken as indicating policies which are necessarily feasible, desirable or deserving of priority at the school level.

Figure 7.1 Elements of schools accountability. *Source*: 'Accountability in the Middle Years of Schooling', East Sussex Accountability Project, in *Calling Education to Account*, McCormick, R. (ed.) © The Open University 1982, reprinted by permission of Heinemann Educational Books, London

is the professional development of teachers and that the central goal is the enhancement of the quality of education for pupils in classrooms. We have discussed elsewhere in this book the skills necessary for leadership and the importance of consultation and collaboration of staff if they are to be committed to the enterprise. The next part of this chapter considers issues of confidentiality, negotiation and ownership which must be faced by those involved in promoting what Barry MacDonald (1976) called 'democratic evaluation'.

Democratic evaluation

The argument for evaluation models which are cooperative and consultative rather than designed and carried out by those 'above' relates to the processes of innovation and change described in Chapter 5. Without participation from the beginning it is likely that the whole exercise will be viewed with suspicion and that any results will be ignored or rejected out of hand. Indeed, without the full cooperation of the teacher(s) it is difficult if not impossible to collect much of the information necessary to classroom-based evaluation (for example, concerning teaching intentions or particular pupils). Additionally, if a teacher has existed in the relatively private world of the classroom for a long time then evaluation in which there is no assurance of confidentiality may result in extreme anxiety and this may affect the teaching itself.

Essentially, evaluation, like any form of staff development, must be regarded as a means of contributing to the continuing development of teacher autonomy. Unilateral decisions taken on the basis of what has been called 'top-down' evaluation are unlikely to have any lasting impact on the quality of teaching and learning in the school. Lawton (1981), in commenting on Barry MacDonald's (1976) three types of evaluation – autocratic, bureaucratic and democratic – provides an interesting diagrammatic contrast which illustrates the essential differences between the 'strict accountability' and 'professional and moral' accountability approaches to evaluation (Figures 7.2 and 7.3).

Whereas in Figure 7.2 the line of answerability is clear, in Figure 7.3 not only is the teacher, for example, responsible to the headteacher but the headteacher is responsible to the teacher. The implication of this is that 'needs' should be jointly identified and priorities negotiated; and that there has to be agreement among staff (if it is a whole-school evaluation) or with an individual member of staff (if it is to be a single-teacher evaluation) as to

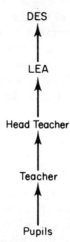

DES

LEA

Head Teacher

Teacher

Pupils

Figure 7.2   Bureaucratic accountability (Lawton 1981). *Source*: Lawton, D., 'Accountability' in Gordon, P. (ed.) (1981) *The Study of the Curriculum*, Batsford

the methods used for collecting information, the use to which the information will be put, and who will have access to both information collected and any ensuing account (i.e. who the 'audience' is). This contract-making is essential, for if staff are going to invest time and energy in evaluation they will need to feel that it is in the interests of, and relevant to, themselves, and/or the pupils and/or the school. Evaluation must therefore (OU 1982):

1. Be fair and perceived as fair by all the parties involved.
2. Be capable of suggesting appropriate remedies.
3. Yield an account that is intelligible to its intended audiences.
4. Be methodologically sound.
5. Be economic in its use of resources (see Chapter 5).
6. Be an acceptable kind of centralized and delegated control.

Establishing an evaluation policy

Essentially, it is the head or deputy who has the responsibility to ensure that evaluation on an individual and institutional level occurs. He or she may not, however, be the evaluator. In many schools evaluation already takes place through such activities as: regular weekly meetings to discuss educational concerns or update knowledge of aspects of the curriculum; working parties to design a new science curriculum, review assessment procedures

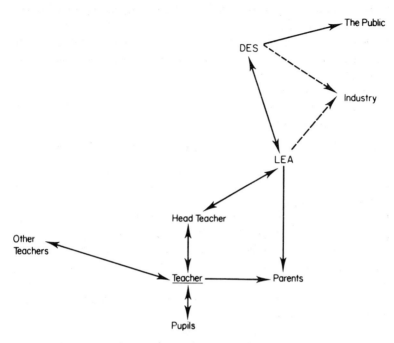

Figure 7.3   Democratic accountability (Lawton 1981). *Source*: Lawton, D., Accountability in Gordon, P. (ed.) *The Study of the Curriculum*, Batsford.

or establish a 'book' policy; visits to other schools and colleagues' classrooms; and, more rarely, active collaboration between schools on aspects of curriculum development. While all these activities, and more, are in addition to traditional forms of in-service work such as course attendance, there are few schools which appear to have an evaluation policy. Let us look now at the kinds of principles which might underpin such a policy, and which arise from the consideration of evaluation made so far in this chapter.

Evaluation principles
1. Evaluation should be regarded as an integral part of professional and curriculum development.
2. Assisted self-evaluation is an effective means of achieving professional development.

3. Evaluation should inform practice.
4. Staff should be involved at all stages in the design, implementation (and evaluation) of evaluation.
5. Evaluation involves the collection of information upon which judgments about past and present work and decisions about future work are based.
6. Evaluation involves a number of different viewpoints. (There are no absolute 'truths', but only partial truths.)
7. Evaluation 'leaders' must ensure confidentiality, accessibility and ownership of information.

Two broad evaluation purposes have been identified. These are:

1. Maintenance – which is directed at 'the preservation and, wherever possible, enhancement of overall levels of performance' (East Sussex Accountability Project 1979).
2. Problem-solving – which is directed at, 'the detection and amelioration of individual points of weakness' (Becher et al. 1981). Whereas maintenance implies general policy review, problem-solving involves working on specific items for change, whether these are curricula, teaching organization and methods, or assessment procedures. In both maintenance and problem-solving, however, the questions which will need to be asked are the same:

Evaluation questions   (Harlen and Elliott 1982, *in* McCormick (1982)).
1. What are the purposes?
2. What information is required for what purpose?
3. What methods can be used to serve those purposes?
4. How should the information be reported?
5. How should the report be used to achieve the original purposes?

Having looked briefly at some of the issues which must be faced by those engaged in evaluation and proposed that, since it is an integral part of professional development, it must form part of a policy for this, let us now look at some of the means which are available for use in assisting whole-school and individual evaluation. There are many more than those described here, but these are intended as examples of good practice. A group of twelve primary schools involved in a collaborative programme emphasized that self-evaluation must (Schools Council 1983):

1. Be based upon clearly specified aims or objectives.
2. Be capable of being adapted to the differing requirements of individual schools.

3. Provide information based on evidence whereby either
   (a) change can be justified, or
   (b) the need for more evidence can be identified.
4. Be capable of involving all members of staff within the school.
5. Be operable within realistic time and resource parameters.
6. Lend itself to obtaining the support and involvement of governors and the authority.
7. Lead to clearly identifiable pupil benefits.

Whole-school evaluation

The next section of this chapter describes briefly three approaches to whole-school evaluation which provide frameworks for action which, in different ways, may be seen as attempting to fulfil these criteria. These are:

1. Local authority self-evaluation/appraisal schemes.
2. *Guidelines for the Review and Internal Development of Schools* (McMahon et al. 1984)
3. *Making School-Centred INSET Work* (OU 1985)

While none of these would claim to be perfect, each offers schools a practical means of establishing and implementing evaluation within the context of a professional development policy.

Local authority self-evaluation schemes

The first thing to note here is that, though the set of guidelines or checklists which make up the schemes are often the result of negotiation between LEA and teacher representatives, the idea has come from the LEA itself. In some LEAs participation in the scheme is obligatory, in others voluntary. In the former case this usually entails formal report to the school governors and the LEA itself. While this holds out the possibility of LEA support in remedying needs which have been identified as a result of the process, it is clear that both professional and contractual accountability are being served.

Given the number of schools in an LEA, and the finite human and financial resources available to provide appropriate support for them, the value of such self-evaluation schemes must be limited. Additionally, the checklists themselves may not be appropriate to the needs of every school – more often than not teachers (other than headteachers) have not been involved in their design. On the other hand, some of these schemes do recognize implicitly that evaluation which is purely by self is limited, and promote the use of Advisers/Inspectors or others as 'auditors' who discuss or check the validity of the evaluation findings and reports. This raises issues of confidentiality and control of information, and may lead to a rhetoric rather than a reality of evaluation. Perhaps a more 'neutral' auditor of reports may be a colleague from a nearby school, Teachers' Centre, university or Institute of Higher Education. Many of these schemes have been surveyed (G. Elliott 1981 and 1982), and the list below (ILEA 1983) provides an illustration of the main headings posed in one such scheme:

1. The children, their parents, the governors and the community.
2. Teaching organization – school staff – responsibility structure – non-teaching staff – staff development.
3. The curriculum – continuity – assessment – extending the curriculum.
4. Organization and management.
5. The building and the general environment.
6. Questions for the individual teacher to ask him or herself.
7. Questions for the headteacher to ask.
8. The future.
9. The acid test. (Would I recommend a colleague to apply for a post at this school? Would I recommend this school to friends for their children?)

Checklists as summarized by the headings above, though useful, are almost always value-laden and their sheer numbers and comprehensiveness can often be daunting for schools. First teachers have to read, digest and interpret meanings, and then select – and there is little, if any, guidance as to how to engage, as a staff, in the process of school self-evaluation. The next two schemes to be described attempt to avoid these problems by concentrating on providing guidelines not only for the organization and content but also for the processes of self-evaluation.

The GRIDS scheme

This scheme is the result of a project established by the Schools Council (now reconstituted as the Schools Curriculum Development Committee) which 'concentrated on assisting whole staffs to carry out a systematic self-review of policy and practice at their school' (McMahon et al. 1984). It is important to note that the project involved collaboration between fifteen primary schools in five LEAs and a university School of Education. The result is materials which contain detailed advice to heads and senior staff on how to conduct a school review and development exercise. One important distinguishing feature is that initially staff are recommended to take a broad rather than detailed look at the school, and 'on the basis of this identify one or two areas that they consider to be priorities for specific review and development, tackle these first, evaluate what they have achieved and then select another priority' (McMahon et al. 1984).

The following extract from GRIDS highlights the key principles underlying the scheme, the importance of the coordinator's role in managing the process of innovation and change, and the outline stages of development:

(a) the aim is to achieve internal school development and not to produce a report for formal accountability purposes;
(b) the main purpose is to move beyond the review stage into development for school improvement;
(c) the staff of the school should be consulted and involved in the review and development process as much as possible;
(d) decisions about what happens to any information or reports produced should rest with the teachers and others concerned;
(e) the head and teachers should decide whether and how to involve the other groups in the school, e.g. pupils, parents, advisers, governors;
(f) outsiders (e.g. external consultants) should be invited to provide help and advice when this seems appropriate;
(g) the demands made on key resources like time, money and skilled personnel should be realistic and feasible for schools and LEAs.
(McMahon et al. 1984)

The authors of GRIDS recognize the problematic nature of review and development work by emphasizing the importance of the provision of a coordinator (whether it be the head or not) whose principal functions are to provide moral and intellectual support as well as to be responsible for progression and continuity. Eight essential tasks are outlined. The coordinator should, (McMahon et al. 1984):

1. Try to ensure that the teachers and others involved feel that the review and development exercise is significant, that the consultation is genuine and that their recommendations will not be ignored.
2. Explain the process clearly to the staff at the outset.
3. Sustain pace and momentum by helping teachers to draw up realistic timetables at each stage and then checking that deadlines are kept.
4. Provide strategic advice where necessary, e.g. how to collect information, what criteria might be used for assessment.
5. Keep a check on what is happening at each stage and advise specific review and development teams if they meet difficulties, e.g. if they cannot decide on a focus for the specific review, fail to meet deadlines, find that some of their recommendations are not feasible.

STAGE 1. GETTING STARTED

1. Decide whether the GRIDS
   method is appropriate
   for your needs.

2. Consult the staff.

3. Decide how to manage the
   review and development.

STAGE 2. INITIAL REVIEW

1. Plan the initial
   review.

2. Prepare and distribute
   basic information.

3. Survey staff opinion.

4. Agree upon priorities
   for specific review
   and development.

STAGE 5. OVERVIEW AND RE-START

1. Plan the overview.

2. Decide whether the changes
   introduced at the development
   stage should be made permanent.

3. Decide whether this approach
   to school review and development should be continued
   or adapted.

happened in the first cycle.

STAGE 3. SPECIFIC REVIEW

1. Plan the specific review.

2. Find out what is the school's present policy/practice on the specific review topic.

3. Decide how effective present policy/ practice actually is.

4. Agree conclusions and recommendations arising from the specific review.

STAGE 4. ACTION FOR DEVELOPMENT

1. Plan the development work.

2. Consider how best to meet the in-service needs of the teachers involved in the development.

3. Move into action.

4. Assess the effectiveness of the development work.

Figure 7.4 The internal review and development process. *Source:* Reproduced with permission of SCDC Publications from *Guidelines for internal review and development in schools: Primary School Handbook.* Longman 1984

6. Contact 'outsiders', e.g. LEA Advisers, teachers from other schools, college lecturers, who might be brought in to provide advice and help at different stages or to organize training courses.
7. Try to ensure that the review and development exercise is both rigorous and systematic.
8. Make some evaluation of the effectiveness of the GRIDS method and whether it achieved what was wanted; the end of the first twelve months may be an appropriate moment.

As with some of the LEA schemes, the project points to the usefulness of outside assistance, but in this case outsiders are called in to assist at appropriate points in the process of the work itself.

Making school-centred INSET work

A third approach to evaluation is contained in materials entitled *Making School-Centred INSET Work* (Easen 1985). These are intended 'to provide practical evidence and support for any teachers who wish to work together in their schools in order to review and develop their pupils' experience of the curriculum', and are aimed also at 'those who are expected to fulfil a "leadership" or "consultancy" function'. As with GRIDS, the ideas and materials were developed in collaboration with teachers in a number of LEAs. Here, however, the similarity ends. The aims are to:

1. Increase your understanding of your own feelings, thoughts and actions in relation to your activity as a teacher within your school.
2. Develop your repertoire of choices for handling both the educational experience provided for the pupils in your school and your relationships with your colleagues.
3. Try out for yourself some of these new ways of handling your professional life.
4. Make decisions about what 'works' and makes sense in relation to your particular school.

(OU 1985)

Through a series of writings and structured activities, the authors provide experiential and reflective frameworks for coping with the challenges of school life, curriculum change (cooperation and conflict), identifying and tackling school problems, collecting information in classrooms, and personal and interpersonal change. The materials are designed to enable each school to work at its own pace on the content which it has chosen to take account of its own priorities. Head, senior staff (there is a guide for group leaders) and teachers can therefore 'dip in' as appropriate to particular parts. Each chapter is organized into reading and practical activity sections. These activities focus on a range of issues concerned with, for example: counselling; creating a less critical amosphere; classroom observation and analysis; breaking down a problem into manageable parts; problem-formulation; feelings engendered by change; humour to relieve tension; effective meetings; etc. While the materials are very different from those of GRIDS and apparently not so straightforward, they do provide uniquely documented insights into the intricate processes of change and changing in which all those engaged in review and development will be involved.

Managing the process

Regardless of the particular scheme adopted, the head or deputy who is managing the process must lay firm foundations. Not only must the school climate be right, but staff must feel secure, and there must be practical support. Figure 7.5 provides a summary of some of the principal issues.

Even then, and regardless of which scheme is adopted, used or modified, success will depend on a number of 'human' factors. Although these have been discussed elsewhere in this book, it is worth restating some of them in the context of this chapter. Clearly it is important for head and staff to agree on the timing of the exercise (the organization of the school needs to be

Aims	Reasons
1. Familiarization with the notion of evaluation	To gain and share information To lower anxieties To generate commitment
2. Establishment of supportive evaluation environments	To facilitate changes in attitudes, values, role definitions and self-images. To foster cooperation
3. Provision of physical and psychological space	To demonstrate support To provide time and somewhere to meet, discuss and work.

Figure 7.5   Preparing for evaluation (Davis 1981)

adaptive and the staff receptive). It is important to allocate human and other resources over an agreed time period to the project as a high priority (this may involve releasing some teachers from other commitments for the duration of the project). It is also necessary for the work to be seen by the teachers as: relevant to perceived need; feasible as well as desirable; uncomplicated but significant; and of ultimate if not immediate benefit to teaching and learning in the classroom. Without the commitment of the staff no amount of careful planning and organization, and monitoring and support, can ensure success. Such commitment is likely to arise in schools where there are a climate and an organizational structure which offer opportunities not only for inter-staff development which focuses on identified school needs but also for individual members of staff to reflect systematically on individual needs – aspects of the teaching and learning in their own classrooms. This too has implications for those in leadership roles, and the next part of this chapter discusses these.

Classroom-based self-evaluation: the teacher as evaluator

> . . . all teachers need help in assessing their own professional performance and in building on their strengths and working on the limitations so identified . . .
> (HMSO 1985)

This statement in a recently published government White Paper implies not only that teachers have a responsibility for evaluating their teaching, but that they also need help in doing so. However, if school-based evaluation is perceived by some teachers as threatening, then evaluation of individual teachers is likely to be much more so. Even self-evaluation is potentially threatening since it inevitably involves self-disclosure, and this is not always welcomed.

The problems of increasing knowledge about practice have been highlighted by Keddie (1971) in her distinction between teacher as educationist and teacher as practitioner:

> . . . while, therefore, some educational aims may be formulated by teachers as educationists, it will not be surprising if 'doctrine' is contradicted by 'commitments' which arise in the situation in which they must act as teachers . . .

And yet from time to time it is essential that life in classrooms is systematically evaluated in some or all of its aspects. Otherwise, curriculum and staff development will always be based on what people say about education and this may not always be the same as what actually occurs.

The justification for ensuring that teachers evaluate their own classroom practice systematically from time to time in order to increase professional effectiveness is based on three assumptions (Day 1981):

1. That teachers cannot be developed (by others) but only given opportunities to develop (for themselves).
2. That effective learning arises in response to the identification and confrontation of 'real' questions by the learner.
3. That decisions about teaching should stem from reflection on the effects of previous actions.

The problem is often that while teachers have the capacity to engage in self-evaluation, they are constrained in the extent to which they may do so by:

1. Practical factors – such as time, energy, skills and resources.
2. Sociological factors – teachers operate within a framework of norms, expectations and values which are often at an implicit level. For example, a new teacher very quickly develops assumptions about practice which allow him or her to cope with the complexities of teaching and being a member of staff. However, since it is relatively unusual for these to be made explicit or tested, the possibilities for evaluating those assumptions which underpin the planning and practice of his or her teaching are minimal.
3. Psychological factors – it is natural to want to live in a world which is constant, which we can control, and which does not threaten our self-esteem. It is not always in our best interests to 'probe' ourselves too much.

There may well be, therefore, a difference between what people say (their intentions or aspirations) and what they do (their practice). It is worth considering the possibility that exhaustive discussions designed to produce documents on the curriculum, aims and objectives, and even job descriptions may produce a rhetoric which is, in varying degrees, inconsistent with the reality of what actually happens in classrooms and schools. It may be much more productive to base such discussions on shared observed and observable experiences of classroom teaching.

An evaluation framework which takes account of both the planning of teaching and teaching itself has been devised by Robert Stake (1967). He divided planning and teaching into three segments:

1. Antecedents – conditions which exist prior to teaching taking place, e.g. pupils' abilities, school and classroom context, resources, teaching organization, etc.
2. Transactions – what happens between pupils and between teacher and pupils during the lesson.
3. Outcomes – what pupils learn (including unintended learning).

Though this was at the time a reaction against the predominance of evaluation which measured only learning outcomes, it also provides a useful model which teachers can use to look at their own teaching; for it draws attention to a logic within the planning which may be different from the logic within the teaching itself, and seeks congruence or match at all levels between intentions and practice. Use of the model allows the teacher to highlight both matches and mismatches between intention and practice. (Figure 7.6)

Let us assume that most teachers have 'a capacity for autonomous professional self-development through systematic self-study, through the study of the work of other teachers and through the testing of ideas by classroom research procedures' (Stenhouse 1975), and that while many already engage in self-study this is not as systematic as it might be. We have considered briefly some of the reasons for this. While most teachers may be described as connoisseurs, able with experience to distinguish, for example, between the significance of different sets of teaching and learning practices, or to recognize and appreciate different facets of their teaching and pupils' learning, they may not find it so easy to be critics who 'disclose the qualities of events or objects that connoisseurship perceives' (Eisner 1979).

The role of the head is crucial here, for it is he or she who must provide opportunities for the development of the connoisseur who is also a critic. Ways in which this may be achieved have been described throughout this book in relation to styles of leadership conducive to promoting curriculum and staff development. Although the ethos or climate of the school will go a long way to minimizing the psychological and sociological constraints described above it is worth remembering that 'the road to educational critique' (MacDonald 1978) may go through several stages and take many years to travel.

At some stage, however, the practical constraints must also be tackled – and it may be argued that this should come sooner rather than later. Heads must provide opportunities for deliberate reflection on classroom practice.

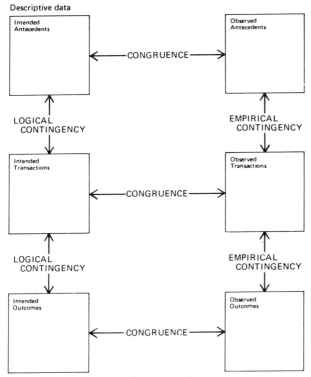

Figure 7.6   An evaluation framework (Stake 1967)

The way in which they might provide these opportunities is through their own knowledge of:

1. The procedures by which teachers may self-evaluate.
2. Techniques which may be used in monitoring classrooms.
3. The means by which teachers may be provided with the moral and intellectual support necessary for self-evaluation.

Evaluation procedures

The six questions in Figure 7.7 have been identified by teachers themselves as being essential for self-evaluation. While these are not listed in order of priority they do focus attention on the three central elements of classroom life – the pupils, the teacher and the task. It is worth noting that while these

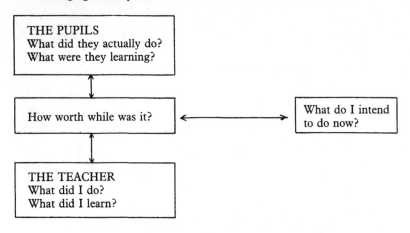

Figure 7.7 Six essential self-evaluation questions. *Source*: The Open University P234 Curriculum in Action: an approach to evaluation, Block 1, 1980

questions inevitably give rise to others (for example, 'How do I find out what the pupils were doing?' or 'What did I intend to do?'), they are designed also to ensure that the teacher moves through four distinct and necessary phases:

1. Description – identifying and selecting events.
2. Interpretation – assessing the consequences of these events.
3. Judgment – assessing how far these events were worth while.
4. Decision – accepting responsibility for 1-3 and planning for future action.

The importance of beginning with description cannot be overemphasized since it ensures that any bias in interpretation, judgments and decisions can be checked against available observed action rather than assumptions or expectations or memories which a teacher might have about the action.

The problems of potential bias will be considered later in the chapter, but before this it is worth while exploring evaluation procedures a little further.

Action research

In order for the teacher to answer the questions posed in Figure 7.7 it will be necessary for him or her to become engaged in action research, which has been defined as the 'study of a social situation with a view to improving the quality of action within it', and as providing 'the necessary link between self-evaluation and professional development' (J. Elliott 1981). Its concern is to 'promote improvement in practice and improvement in understanding simultaneously' (McCormick and James 1983). While this movement originated in America, it has grown in England in the last twenty-five years largely through the efforts of Lawrence Stenhouse (1975 and 1979), John Elliott (1981; Ford Teaching Project 1975) and in Australia through the work of Kemmis et al. (1981) who describe the process of action research as follows:

> In practice, the process begins with a *general idea* that some kind of improvement or change is desirable. In deciding just where to begin in making improvements, one decides on a *field of action* . . . where the battle (not the whole war) should be fought. It is a decision on where it is possible to have an impact. The general idea prompts a '*reconnaissance*' of the circumstances of the field, and fact-finding about them. Having decided on the field and made a preliminary reconnaissance, the action researcher decides on a *general plan* of action. Breaking the general plan down into achievable steps, the action researcher settles on *the first action step*. Before taking this first step the action researcher becomes more circumspect, and devises a way of *monitoring* the effects of the first action step. When it is possible to maintain fact-finding by monitoring the action, the first step is taken. As the step is implemented, new data starts coming in and the effects of the action can be described and *evaluated*. The general plan is then revised in the light of the new information about the field of action and the second action step can be planned along with the appropriate monitoring procedures. The second action step is then implemented, monitored and evaluated; and the spiral of action, monitoring, evaluation and replanning continues.

Elliott (J. 1981) argues that the 'general idea' should be allowed to shift and that 'reconnaissance' should involve analysis in addition to fact-finding. The model he presents is too elaborate to present here, but – as with others introduced in this chapter – should form essential reading for all those with responsibility for promoting the professional development of staff. For the present purposes, however, and before moving on to discuss some of the techniques for collecting classroom observations (as a part of action research) which may be used, here is some practical advice on getting started:

The WHY of observation   Decide what is the purpose. Is it primarily to solve a problem, or to check on the effectiveness of a particular strategy or aspect of curriculum content?

The WHAT of observation   This will be determined by the teachers' own interests, needs or concerns.

Step 1: Choosing the investigation.

Step 2: Asking 'What learning opportunities am I trying to provide?'

Step 3: Deciding on the questions you want to ask.

Step 4: Designing the investigation.
    (a) What data do I need to collect?
    (b) What should be the timing and circumstances of the investigation?
    (c) What techniques should I use?

Step 5: Carrying out the investigation.

Step 6: Analyzing the data.

Step 7: Reflecting on the analysis.

Figure 7.8 Investigating an aspect of teaching (OU 1980). *Source*: The Open University, P234 Curriculum in Action: an approach to evaluation, Block 3, 1980

The WHO of observation Teachers should beware of being over-ambitious. For example, it may be sensible, if pupils are the focus, to observe one pupil or a small group; or if observing self it may be wise to focus on one aspect of teacher talk (e.g. questioning). Figure 7.8 shows an example of a plan for investigating an aspect of teaching.

The WHEN of observation Observation must be built in as a part of the teaching plan, and short concentrated periods of time for this *standing outside* actual contact with pupils may be more practical than long periods when the teacher is likely to be distracted.

The HOW of observation Examples of techniques for collecting observations will be given later in the chapter. It is equally important, however, to find ways of organizing the activity itself so that time and energy can be focused in support of the commitment; and frameworks for recording the information gained from classroom observations must also be devised.

While knowledge of evaluation procedures is important, so also is knowledge of monitoring techniques which will enable teachers to collect, process and reflect upon classroom action.

Classroom monitoring techniques

Elliott (J 1981) has summarized many of the monitoring techniques which are easily available to most teachers, and makes the point that they need to be sufficiently flexible to cater for evidence of the unintended as well as the intended. The list below is our own summary, and while the headings are similar to those used by Elliott, the descriptions are our own unless otherwise indicated.

Document analysis   Teaching plans, syllabi, written work may be analysed.

Impressionistic diaries   of 'observations, feelings, reactions, interpretations, reflections, hunches, hypotheses, and explanations' (Kemmis et al. 1981).

Analytic memos   These are short periodic analyses which consist of 'one's systematic thinking about the evidence one has collected'. (Elliott 1981).

Lesson profiles   which, for example, may record teacher and pupil activity at ten-minute intervals (Walker and Adelman 1975).

Checklists, questionnaires, inventories   These, 'allow one to quantify people's observations, interpretations and attitudes' (J. Elliott 1981) and should be used, if at all, as a means of checking against qualitative judgments.

The running commentary   Here the teacher who is observing an individual or group should write down as much of what he or she hears and observes as possible. This is useful for short periods of observation of at least five minutes.

The shadow study   This is as above, but the recorder is an observer from outside the classroom.

Audio/video recordings and transcripts   Potentially videotape is a most useful means of collecting verbal and non-verbal information. Almost certainly, however, it requires another person to be present and may, initially, cause a distraction in the classroom. However, used sympathetically and over a period of time it can provide by far the richest mine of information (Day 1981). Audio-tape, on the other hand, is easy to use and, though transcription is time-consuming and care has to be taken in attempting to record a group of more than three or four children at work, it provides extremely valuable information.

Interviewing   It is very useful to interview pupils for their responses to a lesson and even more so to have a sympathetic outsider or 'critical friend' (Habermas 1972) do this. The power and authority of a teacher figure must be taken into account when judging the authenticity of pupils' responses, and it is worth while for any outsider to be able to assure them that while general feedback of information to teacher is necessary, individual comments will remain confidential.

Use of an outside observer (who may be a colleague)   A brief example of this is provided later in this chapter. Given a trusting and sympathetic relationship this outside resource or 'third eye' can be invaluable.

Case studies   These essentially provide a set of reflections on the processes of investigation, the results specific to it, and general issues which arise from it. In the context of the individual and the school, such documents may provide reference points for future as well as past work.

As far as possible the techniques used ought to enable one to look at what is going on from a variety of angles or points of view. This is particularly important to those engaged in what is for the most part a qualitative enterprise; for while there is no notion of achieving 'objective' views of classrooms in the narrow, quasi-scientific sense, it is important to provide a subjectively reasoned picture which is internally valid. One means of achieving this is to check 'results' with a colleague and/or pupils, or invite a colleague into the classroom to help decide whether teaching intentions are matched by teaching practices. Another more complicated but potentially more satisfactory and satisfying technique is that of *triangulation*. This is essentially the collecting of 'observations or accounts of a situation (or some aspect of it) from a variety of angles or perspectives and then comparing and contrasting them' (J. Elliott 1981). So pupils, observer and teacher may comment on the same piece of teacher talk, for example, and these comments may be checked for match and mismatch. An added dimension is that these accounts themselves may be checked against the recording of the teacher talk.

Providing moral and intellectual support

It has been implicit throughout this chapter that teachers who are engaged in self-evaluation need support, not only at the beginning, but throughout the process. Self-disclosure may involve considerable anxiety for the teacher and the sympathetic support of colleague(s) must be built in from the beginning. It may also be that the teacher will require practical support (assistance in processing data, use of resources, time, etc) and intellectual support (advice on the design of an observation schedule, the interpretation of a transcript, etc). The likelihood is that the teacher will also need further support in acquiring new skills and knowledge or modifying current skills.

While in-service and consultancy support may be available from the LEA, and this must not be underestimated, it is likely that colleagues in the school will ultimately be the most important single factor in assisting individual teachers in the business of self-evaluation. Their presence as part of a team is necessary to:

1. Establish and sustain a responsive, mutually acceptable dialogue about classroom events and their context.
2. Audit the process rather than the product of possibly biased reporting.
3. Create a situation in which each teacher is obliged to reflect.
4. Act as a resource.

While an 'outsider' can play all of these roles and in addition relieve teachers of the need to gather their own evidence (e.g. tape record themselves, or interview their own pupils), his or her presence is only temporary. Nevertheless, the presence of an outsider who is not employed by the LEA can often provide a unique kind of support for self-evaluation. The final part of this chapter provides an example of the way in which a consultant from outside a primary school assisted in individual classroom-based self-evaluation which led to whole-school professional development. It is by no means as time-consuming as earlier examples of 'action research', and serves to show how even this level of activity – simply being given the opportunity to observe themselves in action over a period of time – can affect both the thinking and practice of teachers.

Case study: individual and whole-school staff development in a primary school

The context for the process of assisted self-evaluation was the desire of the recently appointed headteacher to find an effective way of evaluating the education policy within the school as a whole, and the performance of individual teachers. Having been convinced of the value of self-assessment while still a deputy head, and having been appointed to the school a year previously, she felt that the two way process of trust and acceptance between the staff and herself, and, more importantly, 'the level of friendship and mutual support amongst the teachers themselves' were sufficient to warrant introducing the idea of self-evaluation to the staff. She herself regarded self-evaluation in which teachers could 'identify teaching strategies . . . which are seen to work well, and at the same time perceive those areas of their classroom organization where their teaching skills could be channelled into more productive directions' as an effective means of increasing teachers' awareness of their own performance. She saw video-taping as the best choice, 'since it means a permanent record is available for immediate reaction and feedback, whilst at the same time providing a suitable way of storing material for future review'.

She regarded it as essential that the staff perceived self-evaluation as a 'step forward in their development as professionals and not with any sense of personal threat', and was clear that how far each was able to develop would depend on their experience and attitudes, and 'the trust and respect they have for the people to be involved with them in the project'.

After internal discussions about self-evaluation some of the staff had put forward the opinion that they would welcome help in identifying which classroom practices could be regarded as effective, and which should be adapted or even discarded. This was seen as a necessary precondition for moving towards identifying features of the school in general with a view to changing those which were 'less than satisfactory'. In this project, then, each teacher was filmed in his or her classroom over a period of five weeks for approximately forty minutes each week. The tape was played back to each individual after the 'lesson'. (The headteacher taught the class during this time.) Each teacher chose the focus and, at the end of the sequence, edited the videotape. The edited versions were shared among staff in a series of after-school in-service sessions. In this way teachers were able both to reflect on their own practice and share this with others so that all were able to gain a view of the teaching and learning in other classrooms.

Involving the consultant: first impressions

As the head wrote, the six teachers could be divided into three categories according to their response:

(i) Those who were enthusiastic about the idea from the beginning.

(ii) Those who could appreciate that such an activity would be of considerable value, but who expressed varying degrees of apprehension at the prospect of being filmed.

(iii) Those who were dubious as to the personal benefit to themselves, expressing doubt that such an exercise could improve their performance as teachers.

The level of maturity is bound to be a limiting factor on both the willingness of the individual to engage in self-evaluation and the extent to which the process will be pursued. The case studies confirmed the different attitudes with which the teachers 'entered' the process of self-evaluation. Each had a slightly different motivation and each held different expectations and attitudes. For example, whereas one teacher was sceptical about the benefits to be obtained, but participated because of the 'personal and communal benefit' to be derived from a 'total' school programme, another was enthusiastic to use the opportunity as a means of improving his 'skill and effectiveness' as a teacher. Between those positions were others who were 'very self-protective', 'very nervous' or tentative but 'wanting to improve'. Each of these states of readiness had to be identified, accepted and taken into account in the behaviour of the consultant. It was reasonable to hypothesize that each teacher would 'gain' from the experience in a different way.

A point for consideration in work of this kind is the role of the consultant, and related to this are issues of contract-making and confidentiality.

The role of the consultant

The consultant's role was that of 'independent facilitator', provider of resources, and 'trusted colleague'. Writing about the initial responses expressed by teachers after the first visit, the headteacher stated:

> After meeting with [the consultant] and discovering he was by no means the awesome individual they had envisaged, the remaining worries expressed by one or two teachers were allayed and replaced by confidence in his ability, not only to film appropriate and relevant parts of their classroom activities, but also to help them analyse their teaching techniques and make positive suggestions where necessary.

It is important to highlight the necessity for consultants to take and be seen to take a stance which is independent of those who are seen to be in authority in the work context. To be seen as a pawn of, or in collusion with, the headteacher for example, is potentially to jeopardize the growth of a trusting and therefore open relationship with those not in authority. At the same time, where it is intended that both individual and school needs are served, it is important to accept that different but related contracts with individuals and the headteacher will be established.

Confidentiality and contract-making

There are two interrelated issues here. First, the need for the consultant to establish from the beginning a 'private' relationship with each individual as a basis for building confidence and trust, and second the need of individual teachers or clients to know that whatever is said and whatever information about teaching is collected will be under his or her control. (Will anyone else see the videotapes of classroom teaching? If so, and at what stage?) Care must be taken that those who deliberately place themselves in a 'vulnerable' position where their teaching may be subject to judgment by unknown (or even known) others are reassured of the confidentiality of the material. Like it or not – and it is a sad reflection on the context of teaching and teacher education, not on teachers – there is a general and understandable expectation among teachers that visits by outsiders to their classrooms will often result in negative feedback. Ally this to the 'single loop' (see page 151) private world of learning about practice into which most teachers are placed and in which they spend most of their lives, and the importance of careful and caring negotiation on the issue of confidentiality becomes paramount. Each teacher was assured that only he or she would be present at the initial playback of the videotape of each lesson, that he or she would have control of that information, and that all conversations would be treated as confidential.

In an enterprise in which a number of people give of their time, energy and expertise for a common purpose it is necessary to establish at the outset what each wishes to gain. For although the purpose should be mutually agreed, what each participant will wish to gain from the process may be different. The question of gain is important and is part of the 'practicality ethic' of teachers identified by Doyle and Ponder (1976). They argue that teachers judge the worth of an innovation or 'change in classroom procedure' (such as this project) according to its practical use to them.

The results

The results of the project were, apart from gains which were specific to the classroom practice of each teacher, a perceived increase in self-confidence and critical awareness.

Summary of professional learning issues

John:an increasing confidence in his own critical skills; 'gained enormously as a classroom teacher'; enabled him to improve the quality of his teaching.

Eileen:'reinforces certain points', and made her think deeply about the issues concerned; growth of self-confidence in her own critical abilities.

Linda:'more confident, better organized'.

Anna:after watching the videos she changed her approach to working in and with small groups – with a more satisfactory outcome.

Marian:'it is a good way of studying children'; illustrated, 'strengths and weakness of which I am already aware'.

The learning for the school: one year later

While the scheme was of obvious interest and importance on [the] individual level it would seem to follow that any benefits to be gained by an individual teacher should be transferred to the whole school.
(Headteacher)

The result of the meetings between staff, informally during the work with individual teachers – when one would occasionally be invited to view another's lesson on videotape or 'hear' about the experience in staffroom conversations – and formally in the three after-school in-service meetings agreed for the purpose of sharing practice, can be illustrated by comments written a year later by teachers and the headteacher. Teachers found the comments from other members of staff 'very constructive and illuminating', and that the exercise 'fostered even greater cooperation with each other'. As a staff they had been able 'to observe each other's teaching approaches and learn of different methods and techniques' and enabled to 'gain an overall appreciation of the learning activities pursued in the school from the nursery through the entire primary age range'. They had found the material 'very useful as a basis for staff discussion either on general classroom procedures and techniques or on particular aspects of classroom practice'. They valued the record they now had of 'educational activities, which should benefit any new teacher joining the staff'.

Other detailed comments on their enhanced understandings of the context in which they taught reveal the importance of their sharing experience. All the teachers commented on the value of being able, for the first time, to see a context for their own teaching in which they were able 'to discover our aims and objectives collectively, rather than in isolated areas such as nursery, infant and junior'. As a staff they found that their 'unspoken aims were made clear' to their colleagues as well as themselves. The insights gained into what other classes of older and younger age groups were doing 'helped [us to] plan more effective work and gain a more consistent approach to learning throughout the school'.

These comments from the teachers illustrate the new insights into the curriculum and organization of teaching:

> As an infant teacher I very rarely have the opportunity to see a junior teacher organize her day and teach concepts. It was very interesting and enlightening to see how similar her approach was to mine, within an integrated day.

> It was interesting to see how the progress in child development is maintained and encouraged by teachers' caring attitude; the way the work is presented; the objectives and teaching points upon which the work is based; the natural conclusions following each activity, and to observe how my own work fitted into the overall scheme.

> As I watched my own recordings I realized that much more value could be gained by involving other members of staff; it gave me a source of reference and it gave them a chance to see me at work and to comment favourably or unfavourably, upon what they were watching.

Importantly, in terms of the project aims, they identified the contribution of the work in the process of forming school policy:

> With this view of activities pursued through the school, we have been aided in our formulation of school policy and examination of any curriculum area or teaching technique we may be omitting.

In writing one year after the project had formally ended, the headteacher stated that:

> The benefit gained by individual teachers was proportionate to the amount of effort put into the project – his/her willingness to be self-critical, his ability to identify a situation which required attention, his flexibility in adapting teaching techniques and courage to experiment with changes in organizational and curriculum content.

She pointed to her role with staff who had invited her to view the edited tapes with them, who had 'welcomed comments that were constructive and analytical', and 'sought suggestions as to where changes might be beneficial'. She and the staff as a whole had agreed through discussion that decisions regarding this kind of help should be left to the individual teacher, 'upon whom no external pressure should be brought to bear to share with colleagues more than he/she feels confident to discuss in a public situation'. Earlier in her report she had noted the possible deficiencies of maintaining the principle of self-evaluation in which the individual teacher identifies problems for him or herself and proposes solutions:

> Whilst accepting that this is the ideal situation, it is worth bearing in mind that an individual can make value judgments only with reference to his experience and expertise and if he has the necessary incentive to do so . . .

The point of this brief report of an example of the effects of using an external consultant is to encourage schools to seek outside assistance, but to seek it on their own terms. It also highlights important issues of contracting negotiations and confidentiality, and bias and collaboration, which were raised earlier in this chapter, and with which the chapter will end.

Contracting   There is a need, even when evaluation occurs within the school and is for the school, and no outside sources of help are used, to ensure that issues of time, timing, resource availability and confidentiality of information are negotiated, and agreement is reached before the evaluation begins.

Bias   There is a need to recognize and accept that evaluations are not value-free but, equally, that bias may be minimized by, for example, the use of triangulation techniques (see page 174 and/or the use of auditors, or 'critical friends'.

Collaboration   If there is to be a school policy for professional development which contains as an essential element structured and supported opportunities for individual and group assisted self-evaluation then this must be agreed through discussion and can only flourish if all have an investment in it. Full collaboration in its planning and processes is likely to ensure this.

Those engaged in professional development work have often raised the problem of transferring individual learning to the school context in ways which will influence others. No such problem need arise where the integration of individual and whole-school development is contracted in the initial stages of design (Elliot, J. 1982), and where evaluation is part of an agreed policy for professional development.

References

Argyris, C. and Schon, D.A. (1976) *Theory in practice: increasing professional effectiveness*, San Francisco: Jossey-Bass.

Barnes, D. (1976) *From Communication to Curriculum*, Harmondsworth: Penguin.

Bassey, M. and Hatch, N. (1979) A seven-category interaction analysis for infant teachers to use themselves, *Educational Research*, vol. 21, no.2.

Becher, A., Eraut, M. and Knight, J. (1981) *Policies for Educational Accountability*, London: Heinemann.

Birchenough, M. (1985) *Making School Based Review Work*, NDC Publication, School of Education, University of Bristol.

Cooper, K. (1976) Curriculum Evaluation: Definition and Boundaries, *in* Tawney, D. (ed.) *Curriculum Evaluation Today: Trends and Implications*, Schools Council Research Studies, London: Macmillan Education.

Cronbach, L.J. (1963) Course Improvement through Evaluation, *Teachers College Record*, 64.

Davis, E. (1981) *Teachers as Curriculum Evaluators*, London: George Allen and Unwin.

Day, C.W. (1981) *Classroom-Based In-Service Teacher Education: The Development and Evaluation of a Client-Centred Model*, University of Sussex Education Area, Occasional Paper no.9.

Department of Education and Science (1978) *Primary Education in England: A Survey by HM Inspectors of Schools*, London: HMSO.

Doyle, W. and Ponder, C.A. (1976) The Practicality Ethic in Teacher Decision Making, *Interchange* vol. 8, 1977.

East Sussex Accountability Project (1979) *Accountability in the Middle Years of Schooling: An Analysis of Policy Options*, Brighton: University of Sussex, mimeograph in McCormick, R. (ed.) *Calling Education to Account*, London: Open University/Heinemann Educational Books 1982.

Easen, P. (1985) *Making School-Centred INSET Work*, London: Croom Helm in association with The Open University Press.

Eisner, E.W. (1979) *The Educational Imagination*, West Drayton: Collier Macmillan.

Elliott, G. (1981) *Self Evaluation and the Teacher*, parts 1–3, London: Schools Council.

Elliott, G. (1982) *Self Evaluation and the Teacher*, part 4, London: Schools Council.

Elliott, J. (1973) Is Instruction Outmoded? *Cambridge Journal of Education*, vol. 3, no.3.

Elliott, J. (1978) *Who Should Monitor Performance in Schools?* Mimeo, Cambridge Institute of Education.

Elliott, J. (1981) Action-Research: A Framework for Self-Evaluation in School, Schools Council Programme 2, *Teacher–Pupil Interaction and the Quality of Learning Project*, Cambridge Institute of Education Working Paper no. 1., in

Elliott, J. and Ebbutt, D (eds), *Facilitating Action Research in Schools*, Falmer Press (forthcoming).

Elliott, J. (1982) Institutionalizing Action Research in Schools, *in* Elliott, J. and Whitehead, D. (eds.) *Action Research for Professional Development and Improvement of Schools* 5, Cambridge: CARN Publications.

Ford Teaching Project (1975) Unit 2: *Research Methods: Ways of doing research in one's own classroom*, CARE, University of East Anglia.

Galton, M. and Simon, B. (eds.) (1980) *Progress and Performance in the Primary Classroom*, London: Routledge and Kegan Paul.

Habermas, J. (1972) *Knowledge and Human Interest*, London: Heinemann.

Harlen, W. and Elliott, J. (1982) A Checklist for Planning or Reviewing an Evaluation, *in* McCormick, R. (ed.) *Calling Education to Account*, London: Heinemann Educational.

HMSO (1985) *Better Schools*, Government White Paper.

House, E. (1972) The Conscience of Educational Evaluation, *Teachers College Record*, vol. 73, no.3.

Inner London Education Authority (1983) *Keeping the School Under Review*, London: ILEA.

Keddie, N. (1971) Classroom Knowledge *in* Young, M.F.D. (ed.) *Knowledge and Control*, Middx: Collier-Macmillan.

Kemmis, S. et al. (1981) *The Action Research Planner*, Geelong, Victoria: Deakin University Press, Open Campus Program.

Lawton, D. (1981) Accountability *in* Gordon, P. (ed.) *The Study of the Curriculum*, Batsford Studies in Education.

Macdonald, B. (1976) Evaluation and the Control of Education *in* Tawney, D. (ed.) *Curriculum Evaluation Today: Trends and Implications*, Schools Council Research Studies, Macmillan Education.

MacDonald, B. (1978) Accountability, standards and the process of schooling, *in* Becher, A. and Maclure, S. (eds.) *Accountability in Education*, Windsor: NFER Publishing.

McCormick, R (ed) (1982) *Calling Education to Account*, Open University/Heinemann Educational Books: London.

McCormick, R. and James, M. (1983) *Curriculum Evaluation in Schools*, Croom Helm Ltd.

McMahon, A. et al. (1984) *Guidelines for the Review and Internal Development of Schools: Primary School Handbook*, Schools Council/Longman.

Nuttall, D. (1981) *School Self-Evaluation: Accountability with a Human Face?* London: Schools Council.

Open University (1980) *Curriculum in action: an approach to evaluation*, P234, Block 3, Milton Keynes: Open University Press.

Open University (1982) *Curriculum Evaluation and Assessment in Educational Institutions*, E364, Block 1, Milton Keynes: Open University Press.

Peters, R.S. (1968) Must an Educator Have an Aim? *in* Peters, R.S. (ed.) *Concepts of Teaching*, London and Windsor: Macmillan and Nelson, USA: Rand McNally & Co.

Schools Council (1983) *Primary Practice* Working Paper 75, Methuen Educational.

Schulman, L.S. and Keisler, E.R. (eds.) (1966) *Learning by Discovery: A Critical Appraisal*, Chicago: Rand McNally & Co.

Sharp, R. and Green, A. (1975) *Education and Social Control*, London: Routledge and Kegan Paul.

Simons, H. (1981) Process Evaluation in Schools, *in* Lacey, C. and Lawton, D. (eds.) *Issues in Evaluation and Accountability*, London: Methuen and Company.

Stake, R.E. (1967) The Countenance of Educational Evaluation, *Teachers' College Record*, 68.

Stake, R.E. (1969) Language, Rationality and Assessment *in* Beatty, W.H. (ed.) *Improving Educational Assessment and an Inventory of Measures for Affective Behaviour*, Washington, D.C.: Association for Supervision and Curriculum Development.

Stenhouse, L. (1975) *An Introduction to Curriculum Research and Development*, London: Heinemann Educational.

Stenhouse, L. (1979) *What is action-research?* CARE, University of East Anglia (mimeograph)

Walker, R. and Adelman, C. (1975) *Guide to Classroom Observation*, London: Methuen.

Note:　Figure 7.6. An evaluation framework. *Source*: Stake, R.E. (1969) Language Rationality and Assessment, in Beatty, W.H. (ed.) *Improving Educational Assessment and in Inventory of Measures of Affective Behaviour*. Reprinted with permission of the Association for Supervision and Curriculum Development. © (1969) by the Association for Supervision and Curriculum Development. All rights reserved.

CHAPTER 8

DEVELOPING RELATIONSHIPS WITH PARENTS AND GOVERNORS

Our final chapter provides some suggestions on how the head can communicate with those people who are external to the school but likely to have some form of relationship with, and increasingly influence upon, the people working in it. It can no longer be assumed that the public will support a school simply because the building exists. Today, schools must gain support through good performance and a well-thought-out information service. The head cannot be the sole spokesperson for the school. The entire staff, pupils, and the school itself must all become vehicles of information to all groups associated with supporting the life of the school. The successful primary head is the one who knows how to capitalize on the interest of all those involved with the school and to turn their involvement into a positive force in the school. Developing relationships is all about the head and staff understanding the roles, expectations and needs of all those who make up the wider community associated with any single school community.

While it is true that the head must take into account both the resources available, and the expressed needs of others in the home–school partnership, it is also true that effective management requires not only a knowledge and understanding of what 'is' but a clear and acute vision of what 'might' be – of what is desired. Without such a vision, school management is likely to degenerate into little more than a set of techniques designed to minimize difficulties and lead to a less hectic life. An essential ingredient for the effective development of relationships with parents, therefore, is a clear and articulate philosophy of education with respect to the desired relations between the home and the school; for without this the head has no criteria by which to decide between opposing possibilities. For this reason, it is important that both heads and teachers identify possible philosophies of home–school relationships, and make conscious choices between these on the basis of some clear and coherent set of values. Unless primary heads know where they stand and can communicate their ideas successfully, it is unlikely that they will do more than confuse others.

There is no set of clear and unequivocal 'answers' to major questions on how to work effectively with parents and governors, because the solution to a problem has to be found in that situation and not imported from outside that school's environment. It is a skill required by the head, as leader, to have the insight to be able to identify the most important factors in a situation; and to be able to relate these factors in such a way that an answer is found for that situation.

The role of the primary head

The position of the primary head in this country remains a powerful one, in spite of the many social, political and economic changes which have taken place during the last two decades. The changes have made the role of the present-day head a more demanding and complex one than ever before, and have highlighted the head's need to form and develop a whole range of relationships. Managing any relationship successfully requires considerable ability and a wide range of personal skills, particularly the ability to listen carefully and be sensitive to the needs of others.

The head is, in fact, at the centre of a web of relationships. Each member of the head's role set – governors, parents, teachers – has expectations as to how the head should perform the role. It is essential, therefore, that he or she should not only have thought through issues very carefully, but be efficient at communicating those thoughts to others and listening to their opinions and questions.

In recent years, primary heads have been led by official information from the DES in the form of the Taylor Report (1977), Circular 15/77 (1977), and Circular 6/81 (1981), to question the nature of their role in relation to maintaining external relationships. The Great Debate initiated by the Prime Minister in 1976 gave rise to the notion that schools should be organized so as to provide a framework of consent and accountability. The message is quite clear – a head cannot run an effective school without taking into consideration the views of teachers, governors and parents. This demands a serious consideration of the role that heads must play if they wish to retain the support of those with whom they have to work. To some heads this may seem a threat to their professional territory, and they may worry that influential minorities will begin to dominate schools and undermine their efforts. Heads who have traditionally regarded themselves as the only influence over the curriculum and relationships with parents may well feel very threatened by the events of recent years. Yet to ignore these developments is unwise.

Heads ought to ask themselves, 'How can I gain the full support of the local community, parents and governors whose understanding of primary education may be outdated and ill informed?' and 'How can all those people who are in any way associated with this school share with me the responsibility of providing the best possible education for the children?' Primary schools in the final two decades of the twentieth century have to be more open, accountable to and cooperative with the wide community, which may require some heads to change their attitudes towards the patterns of authority and influence which have long been established. The change has, in fact, been willed by the government and although it may be difficult for some heads to accept in practice, there can be no avoiding the need for the head to examine methods of managing the school in order to discharge effectively all the responsibilities towards the parents and governors.

Relationships with parents: some initial considerations

In formulating any policy concerning the relationship of the school to the parents of its pupils, and in implementing such a policy, heads and all staff must bear in mind a number of considerations, especially an awareness of the needs of others and possible resource implications.

Needs

Central to any consideration of home–school relations is the question of the needs of pupils, teachers and the community itself. These needs are important in at least two main ways. On the one hand, many of these needs are of considerable importance in providing objectives for the school – the school exists partly in order to go some way towards meeting the needs of pupils. On the other hand, the needs which people have act as powerful motivators for them, influencing what they consider to be important, what is considered worth striving for, and ways in which people react to various ideas. Without some understanding of how people are motivated it is difficult for the head to identify what are likely to be successful strategies and programmes in relating the school and the home.

An awareness of needs supplies, in a specific situation, a sort of checklist of questions which can be asked, with the purpose of sensitizing the head to what may be important dynamics of a situation. Thus, when faced with a 'difficult' parent, it is worth stopping to consider such questions as:

1. What need is this parent meeting in acting this way?
2. What needs am I meeting in acting as I am?
3. Has this parent needs in this situation which are obviously legitimate, and which I can assist in meeting?
4. Am I working with this parent in such a way that the parent is reassured about the school, and will be welcome on future occasions? Is the parent only likely to be welcome if certain approved behaviours are exhibited?

Any consideration of the needs and interests of children, parents, teachers and the community must take account of potential conflicts. Not all parents want the same things and some of them want conflicting things, e.g. different styles of classroom discipline. Within a single staffroom teachers will have different needs, interests and concerns. This is often expressed by heads as a worry about the motivation of staff. Whatever the cause, and whatever the form any differences may take, such potential conflicts make considerable demands on the skills, patience and sympathy of the head.

In planning to identify and meet the needs of parents it must be recognized that quite often teachers themselves, and the profession as a whole, have had a vested interest in establishing certain kinds of relationships with parents. This is often expressed by teachers as a fear of 'parent power' and was inherent in many reactions to the Taylor Report (DES 1977). So when there are discussions about the partnership between parents and teachers, there is not always the assumption that what is being talked about is an equal partnership.

It is important, in practice, to sort the various needs into an order of priority. Given that time is always a limited resource, it is essential that priorities be clearly established. Upon what basis can this reasonably be done? The great temptation is that heads will accept all needs as legitimate, but actually do what they would have done anyway – on the grounds that while all needs are legitimate, a certain set are either the most important, or the most readily met, or the most urgent. So, in practice, the good can indeed be the enemy of the best.

Resources

Any proposal to develop relationships with parents is likely to have resource implications – to involve the expenditure of some sort of resource. Typically, in schools, when we hear the word 'resource' we think first of money; but when considering home–school relationships there are more likely to be other resources of greater importance, for example:

Time A most valuable and very scarce resource. How much time is available? Where? Will they want to spend it in that way?

Goodwill Again a valuable resource, often not noticed until it is missing. This is related to:

Reputation If the head has a good reputation for meeting important needs, for being efficient and effective, then it is most likely that some innovation can take place. Innovation often involves asking other people to trust you as together you venture into the unknown. A reputation for usually being 'right' is a valuable start to people trusting you, although under some circumstances this can also work against the head!

People The most important resource of all. All who are to be involved must be seen very positively as resources which can be organized and developed, resources without which the programme cannot happen, and without which no leader can be effective. Careful consideration must be given not only to their needs, but to their relationships, hopes and aspirations. The success of a programme of home–school relationships will depend on the skill of the head to develop such a programme so that all the people involved continue to be willing participants.

Action strategies for developing relationships with parents

Informing the parents

Since the publication of the Plowden Report in 1967 (Central Advisory Council for Education 1967), primary schools have made great efforts to follow the recommendations by keeping parents better informed. After all the advice from the DES over many years as to what schools ought to inform parents about, and how this may be attempted, it is indicative of present trends that it is now a statutory obligation for detailed written information about the school to be published annually. The East Sussex Accountability Project (Cleave et al. 1982) suggests that many parents' views of school are based on misunderstanding, ignorance, fears and fantasies which can easily be increased rather than decreased by what teachers say and do! The researchers point out that most parents in their survey had no means of reassuring themselves that gloomy rumours about present-day education did not apply to their local school, while such false accusations only made teachers more defensive. The study emphasizes that what parents really want is more information on their child, the methods of teaching and classroom organization.

How does the head know that the information provided by the school matches the needs of parents – tells them what they want to know? The head and staff must be conscious of the need to question parents on issues which affect the children's education. As well as the personal contact it may be appropriate for the school to produce a questionnaire for parents to complete about the practices employed within the school. Perhaps the parent governor could assist with the compilation of such a document. Only when genuine attempts have been introduced to investigate parental opinion thoroughly can the head begin to develop real and lasting home–school relationships. Some of the main strategies for informing parents are likely to be:

The school brochure   Don't just provide the minimum information which by law must be presented. Tell parents about such things as school finance, the powers of the governing body, the role of the parent governor, how children and work are organized, what is kept in children's records, and the full yearly programme of school events. The brochure should be available to all parents and the wider community. Heads should make it available in local libraries, clinics, churches and community centres.

The newsletter   A monthly newsletter can help the parents make sense of what the children may tell them about various class or school activities. In addition it can provide up-to-date announcements about meetings, courses staff are attending, parents' functions and particular achievements. It can also contain children's poems, imaginative stories and accounts of recent happenings. An advertisement column may add to its interest.

The noticeboard   This will probably serve many of the functions of the newsletter but be big enough to contain examples of children's original art and story work. There may be enough space to give greater details on classroom organization and teaching methods. Some space can be left for parents to use to advertise local events.

Parents' meetings Relate these to the children's education but before beginning find out what the parents would like to discuss. Don't make the meetings too large. An informal atmosphere gives parents and teachers time to talk about individual children. Avoid outside speakers – plan workshop sessions when parents have an opportunity to participate in practical learning situations similar to those undertaken by the children. Involve the children where appropriate – they can be a great help with necessary explanations. Try to provide some written statement for parents to take away to read at leisure. If coffee mornings are held, provide a crêche for pre-school children in order to maximize the parent response.

Visits to the classroom Most parents are keen to understand the teachers' methods. Parents can be invited in small groups at predetermined times to see the children at work – these may be termly, fortnightly or weekly, depending on local circumstances. Experience suggests that parents will make a special effort to see the 'class assembly'.

Consultations Individual consultations between parent and teacher probably provide the single most important opportunity for parents to find out about their children's progress and how best to help them. Give parents a choice of appointment times and make sure the time allowed is long enough to discuss the child in detail – be a good listener. Ensure that such consultations are in private. The children's work should be available on the day before the consultation for parents to collect and browse through at home – this will provide a firm basis for discussion.

Unless the consultation time is used wisely by teachers and heads, the parent may be more alienated than helped by such meetings. To help teachers prepare for such consultations ask them to observe these *don'ts*:

1. Don't let your desk form a barricade between you and the parent. Encourage the parent to join you sitting around a table or on easy chairs in the head's office.
2. Don't confuse parents with too many suggestions at any one time. Concentrate on one or two things they can do to help their child at home. Emphasize important points.

3. Don't display disapproval. Any sign that you disapprove of what a parent is saying or doing may make him or her stop talking and listening.
4. Don't pry or ask questions if the parent appears reluctant to discuss personal matters.
5. Don't assume that parents want your advice. Many come to school only because they think it is their duty. If you give the impression that they need help, they will see it as disapproval and criticism.
6. Don't generalize or sound vague. Always try to be concrete in your suggestions and specific about the areas of weakness.

There are ways in which the head can also help parents prepare for a parent–teacher consultation in advance, especially by producing some guidelines for parents. These suggestions can appear in the school brochure or may be sent home a few days prior to a meeting:

1. Ask your child if there is anything he or she would like you to discuss with the teacher.
2. Decide in advance the questions you want to ask the teacher. It is a good idea to write them down.
3. Be ready to tell the teacher a little bit about your child's home life. The school wants to know about your child's hobbies, interests and feelings. Knowing these things will be helpful in the teaching approach to your child in school.
4. If you are concerned about a rumour you have heard, or something your child has told you about his or her class or teacher, then ask about it at the consultation.
5. Be reasonable in what you expect the teacher to do and the amount of special attention your child can receive. Ask how you can meet some of the child's needs at home.
6. A phone call or visit to your child's teacher will set up an appointment at a time convenient to both of you.

Programmes designed to involve parents are only worth while if put into practice, and may be negated by one seemingly insignificant oversight by a well-intentioned member of staff or even by the head! The list of suggestions below may help the head reflect upon current parent relations.

1. Be aware of your manner when greeting parents as they enter the school. Do you greet them with the words, 'Can I help you?' in a tone of voice indicating something akin to, 'What are you doing here?'
2. Provide comfortable chairs for those who have to wait. Ensure that the

waiting area is aesthetically pleasing, with plants and flowers a regular feature. A school brochure and examples of children's imaginative stories can also be on display.

3. Show new parents around the building and introduce them to their child's teacher. Talk with them in private about the school and encourage them to talk with you about their child without constantly bombarding them with questions.

4. Reporting bad news to parents is never easy but is far better received if done personally. So try not to resort to the typewriter before the telephone to initiate contact, and where at all possible encourage a meeting to talk things over. It may be that the school is not the best place for this.

5. When parent's evenings/days are being held, circulate amongst the parents and chat to as many as you possibly can. Those parents who really wish to talk with you will soon search you out!

6. When a family move from your area, present them with a farewell questionnaire about the school. The parting comments of parents can be very revealing.

The six suggestions outlined are all within any head's ability.

Heads often assume that every parent knows of their availability. Because a few parents come into school frequently it is assumed that every parent knows just how to contact them. Parents do not automatically know how to contact the head; they do not know whether he or she welcomes phone calls from them on routine matters, and if they are new to the school they don't know the many kinds of activities in which they are welcome to get involved. Early in the school year the head should urge parents to do the following:

1. Contact the school when a problem arises or when a crisis occurs at home which may affect the child.

2. Bring any special talent or skill they may have to the knowledge of their child's teacher.

3. Let you know when a child is enthusiastic about a class project or seems to be having particular difficulty with one.

4. Contact the school to check out the facts when they hear a rumour from their child or from a neighbour.

5. Offer their services as a volunteer helper.

Involving the parents

The NFER Survey *Parental Involvement in the Primary School* (Cyster et al.

1980), which examined the practice in primary schools ten years after the Plowden Report (Central Advisory Council for Education 1967), suggests that any progress towards involving parents during the working day must be treated cautiously. Parents helping in the school are not the key method of building good home–school relationships, not only because the proportion of parents likely to be involved in this way is small but because of the pressures placed on heads and teachers. However, the implications of the early intervention studies (Armstrong and Brown 1979) are that there are likely to be beneficial long-term effects on parents' views of education and of their role in relation to their children's development when the school, parents and children work together. Parents should be viewed as educators, with a role to play in their child's development – their participation should be active, working directly with children, whether at home or in school.

There are three good reasons why it is important to involve parents as working partners. First, when parents work in the school they gain first-hand experience and a degree of insight into how the school functions, and therefore a firmer basis on which to discuss their child's education. Second, parents working in the school, are able to offer a wide range of skills and interests which otherwise might not be available. Third, it is likely that the parents will become good 'public relations' officers for the school. This was borne out in the East Sussex Accountability Project (Cleave et al. 1982) which reported that those mothers who were allowed to help in the classroom were noticeably better informed than others and often radically changed their opinions to become strong supporters of the school's activities.

Parents can be an important resource in the life of the school and are often underutilized. However, not all parents can, or want, to work in the school and not all schools would find it easy to accommodate large numbers of parents during the day. Organizing parents as partners is no easy matter, and there is a need to consider a series of planned developments before a programme can become effective. The head is likely to play four different yet essential roles:

1. Initiator The head must set up staff discussion in order that the needs, interests and concerns of the teachers can be identified. There is little point in parents becoming involved unless the teachers have a clear perception of the role of parents, recognize their possible needs, and are willing to recognize the potential benefits to the school. A number of key questions need to be answered. How can the parents' contributions best be utilized throughout the school and in individual classrooms? How many parents can be accommodated? What times of day are most suitable? How regular a commitment is required, or can reasonably be expected? Do all the teachers have to be involved initially?

2. Promoter   The head must give all parents the opportunity to offer regular help to the school. An invitation should be sent to the parents asking them to respond if at all possible, requesting information about what they would be interested in doing, and inviting them to an initial meeting with the head and class teacher. It is important that a list of activities is drawn up by the teacher and publicized, so that there can be a matching of teachers' needs and parents' skills or interests.

3. Controller   The head must make it clear whether regular or occasional help is wanted and whether or not parents may come to help without prior notice. It is preferable to work towards planned regular help so that the teacher can communicate to parents the aim of the activity and how to deal with any difficulties over either the task or matters of discipline.

4. Maintainer   The head must ensure through frequent discussion with teachers and parents that the partnership is able to develop. Parents must feel welcome in the school, and should be provided with refreshments at break times, when they can meet either with the other parents or informally with the staff for discussion. The teacher's first task is to attend to the children. It may be that the involvement in the classroom of certain parents could present difficulties to the teacher, or to the children of those parents, and therefore this should be carefully explained to such parents. Some teachers will be unhappy with parents as partners in the classroom, but may be amenable to accepting other kinds of help, for example in the preparation of teaching resources in an area away from the parent's own children. Experience suggests that the assistance of some parents in the classroom can be a valuable asset, but only at the teacher's instigation. If there are teachers who lack the confidence or experience to be involved with parents, then it is important not to rush into any partnership, but to build up a new situation gradually.

Relationships with governors

It is understandable, given the educational climate which existed in the mid

1970s, and the conflict about the teaching methods to be used, that there was at that time a need for improved communication between the primary school and the home, if parents were to maintain confidence in the education system. The demise of the eleven-plus examination, and the introduction of the 'learning by discovery' methods rather than 'rote', both of which developments were given ample media coverage, led to a demand amongst parents for wider participation in the life of the school. This pressure led in 1975 to the setting up of the Taylor Committee to consider the role of the school managers and governors. The view seemed to be that the power held by the school over the curriculum should be subject to the consent of those affected by the consequences of the decisions taken by the school.

The Taylor Report, *A New Partnership for Our Schools* (DES 1977) fully investigated parental involvement and the role which the school should play. Parents were recognized as having a need for adequate communication:

> The Governing body should satisfy itself that adequate arrangements are made to inform parents, to involve them in their children's progress and welfare, to enlist their support, and to ensure their access to the school and teachers by reasonable arrangement.

In addition to their general responsibility for the wellbeing of the school and for good relationships, the governors, said the Report, should establish the school's aims, share in the formation of a programme for achieving them, keep the school's progress towards them under continuous review, and make periodic and more formal appraisals of that progress.

For many heads the recommendations of the Taylor Report were far-reaching and not all have found them either acceptable or easy to operate. However, since the publication of the Report, some of the recommendations have been enforced by statutory measures which should as a result have led heads to review existing practices and the relationships between the governors, parents and the community at large.

All primary schools have a formally constituted governing body which needs to be kept well informed by the head on all matters relating to the school's organization, curriculum, allocation of resources, progress and general activities. The school governors are likely to meet at least once each term, when the head should present a written report outlining all the details of school life which will help the governors have a clear insight into the workings of the school. In order that each governor can come to the meeting fully aware of recent school developments it is very important that the head's written report is circulated to governors at least 7 – 10 days before a formal meeting. In this way people can think in some detail about issues they may wish to comment upon, thus enabling the meetings to be more purposeful and relevant to the needs and interests of those associated with the local community.

The headteacher's report to the governors

There are a variety of styles which can be adopted by the head in presenting a written report – the outline suggested below sets out the school's development under ten main headings. The headings can be used as a basis for each report although certain items listed under them may only require comment at specific times during the school year.

1. Pupils   Number on roll; class organization and size (in some schools this may only be necessary at the start of each school year); comparison with numbers on roll over the last 2–3 years at a similar stage in the school year; future numbers – falling/rising roll implications; a general statement of attendance; a general statement of lunches/sandwiches where it varies from the norm.

2. Staffing: teaching and non-teaching   The teaching complement at the start of the academic year with any relevant details on teachers with posts of special responsibility; new appointments; resignation, with reasons; absence, with reasons.

3. Curriculum/organizational developments   Any relevant comments on particular developments such as specific projects or new approaches; assessment and testing; changes in teaching/class organization; capitation – report on annual expenditure; educational visits; courses attended by staff.

4. Extracurricular activities   Special events such as plays and concerts; news of clubs and societies; information on any inter-school activities.

5. Parental involvement   Activities organized by the school and any form of parent association.

6. Buildings   Repairs; improvements; furnishing and equipment; the general appearance of the school building and surrounds; anticipated future needs.

7. Health and safety   Visits of school nurse, dentist, doctor, etc; a report on termly fire drill; any matter relating to general health and safety.

8. Visitors   Details of any special visitors to the school.

9. Special items   Requests for leave of absence; requests for secondment; requests for occasional holidays; a review of special needs that cannot be met within the school allowance.

10. Future events   Dates of activities that are taking place in the school in the months before the next governors' meeting.

It is always wise for the head to have talked prior to the meeting with the chairman of governors about any item in the head's report on the agenda which may need clarification, or points which it is thought may give rise to debate amongst the governing body. There will be times during the year when it may be appropriate to give the governors the opportunity to be fully informed in depth on specific aspects of curriculum development, when by invitation other members of staff can join a governors' meeting either to talk to the governors or to run a short workshop session. It is important that such sessions are planned well in advance by the head and staff so that every attempt is made to involve all governors actively in the learning process. Although all governors' meetings have an air of formality about them the head should make every effort to help people feel comfortable and relaxed in the school setting. Each governor should be greeted on arrival, when tea or coffee can be available for those who require refreshment. The arrangement of furniture should allow for relaxed seating with no large tables as barriers between various groups within the room. Some spare pencils and paper could be at hand for those who come without them, so that they can keep notes of any particular points of interest.

The chairman of governors should be kept regularly informed between meetings of developments within the school which fall within the jurisdiction of the governing body. Indeed, keeping in frequent contact with the chairman throughout the school year is a most important and necessary role that the head must play to ensure that decisions and information affecting the school are fully shared. There should also be many opportunities for the governors to be invited to the school for a whole range of functions which will provide them with the chance to see pupils at work, talk to the staff, and meet the parents. The five points below will act as a reminder of some of the times when governors may wish to visit the school:

1. At any time during the school day to gain some experience of the processes by which children learn and teachers teach.
2. At specific times when aspects of the curriculum are being developed which may add a new dimension to the work of the school.
3. All parents' evenings or open days when children's work will be on display and parents will be visiting the school.
4. When any curriculum activity is held to inform parents of the methods used to teach the children.
5. All concerts or special productions when the children will be demonstrating their various talents.

It may be that not all governors accept such invitations, but it is essential that they are invited to play their part in the integral life of the school, so that they can have the chance to carry out their assigned responsibilities with as much information about the school as possible. Whilst all governors may not be fully versed in all that is involved in good primary practice there will be many who are likely to have considerable knowledge about education in general, and whose level of interest is very high indeed. The head must always be seeking to keep the channels of communication with the governors completely open, thus avoiding the criticism that the 'professionals' are not prepared to share working ideas and practices.

References

Armstrong, G. and Brown, F. (1979) *Five Years On: A Follow Up Study of the Long Term Effects on Parents and Children of an Early Learning Programme in the Home*, Oxford: Social Evaluation Unit.

Central Advisory Council for Education (England) (1967) *Children and Their Primary Schools* (The Plowden Report) vol. 1, London: HMSO.

Cleave, S., Jowett, S. and Bate, M. (1982) *And So to School*, Slough: NFER, Nelson.

Cyster, R., Clift, P.S. and Battle, S. (1980) *Parental Involvement in the Primary School*, Slough: NFER.

Department of Education and Science (1977) *A New Partnership For Our Schools* (The Taylor Report) London: HMSO.

Department of Education and Science (1977) *Information for Parents*, Circular 15/77, London: HMSO.

Department of Education and Science (1981) *The School Curriculum*, Circular 6/81, London: HMSO.

INDEX